Collins *gem*

Garden Wildlife

D0765885

How to encourage and attract
wildlife into your garden

MICHAEL CHINERY

First published in 2006 by
Collins, an imprint of
HarperCollins*Publishers*
77–85 Fulham Palace Road
Hammersmith, London W6 8JB

The Collins website address is: www.collins.co.uk

Collins Gem® is a registered trademark of
HarperCollins Publishers Limited.

07 09 11 10 08 06
2 4 6 5 3 1
© Michael Chinery, 2006

A catalogue record for this book is available from the British Library

Created by: SP Creative Design
Editor: Heather Thomas
Designer: Rolando Ugolini

The publishers would like to thank CJ Wildbird Foods for their kind
assistance in providing many of the photographs of their bird and
animal products. For further information go to: www.birdfood.co.uk

ISBN-13: 978 0 00 720990 3
ISBN-10: 0 00 720990 8

Colour reproduction by Digital Imaging
Printed and bound by Amadeus s.r.l., Italy

CONTENTS

PART ONE

The garden habitat

Today's gardens are our most important nature reserves. In some areas, they are undoubtedly more important for wildlife than the surrounding 'countryside', with its pesticide-drenched monocultures. This is true even where the gardener does nothing in particular to encourage visitors: the wide range of plants grown in a typical garden is itself enough to attract lots of insects, and the insects bring in the birds. By being more laid-back and a little less tidy, you can have a garden buzzing with wildlife and filled with tasty crops and fine flowers. Your guests will actually do much of the pest control for you – free of charge!

A colourful wildlife garden
Wildlife gardens aim to increase the number of native species visiting and residing in a garden without any loss of productivity.

GARDEN DIVERSITY

Although we may refer to the garden as a single habitat, on a par with a woodland or a meadow, most gardens are complex mixtures of habitats, supporting their own rich assemblage of plant and animal life.

MICRO-HABITATS

The flower border, a major feature of most gardens, contains a wide range of plants that flower at different times and attract insects and other small

Even the smallest of backyards in an urban area can still be a riot of colour, packed with flowers that act as filling stations for butterflies and many other insects.

A single climbing rose can feed a huge number of insects, which, in turn, can provide food for numerous spiders and birds. The birds may also nest there, well protected from predators by the rose's prickly stems.

creatures for much of the year. Caterpillars chew the leaves, bugs suck the sap, bees and butterflies feast on the nectar, and many other insects attack the fruits and seeds. Hidden from view, the roots provide sustenance for wireworms, leatherjackets, slugs and millipedes. Earthworms derive most of their nourishment from the decaying plant matter in the soil. All these creatures provide food for birds and small mammals, so even a simple flower border is a mixture of several micro-habitats.

Tiny mosses, seen here covered with pear-shaped spore capsules, erupt from the smallest cracks in walls and paths.

Vegetable plots

The vegetable plot has a similar diversity to that of the flower border, although it does not have much in the way of nectar sources and, being subject to more disturbance as crops are planted and harvested, it tends to support a smaller variety of animal life.

Trees, shrubberies and hedges

These lend welcome shade and shelter to other parts of the garden and are micro-habitats in their own right, providing homes and hunting grounds for insects, spiders, birds and many other creatures.

Walls, fences and paths

These provide yet more living space for both flora and fauna, a fact that is easily appreciated when you look at the number of spider webs that adorn the fences in the autumn. Even ordinary concrete paths can support wildlife – tiny mosses wedge themselves into cracks in the concrete, while ants often nest underneath the paths and benefit from the heat absorbed by the concrete on sunny days. You might not even know that they are there until they fly off on their marriage flights in the summer.

Garden ponds

A pond is one of the richest of all wildlife habitats, and garden ponds, happily, are now becoming

Having been hit by the disappearance of so many farm and village ponds, many frogs now find refuge in our garden ponds and mop up the slugs in return for the hospitality.

increasingly popular. Pond-watching can be great fun, and the garden pond can literally be a life-saver for frogs, toads and dragonflies, all of which are now suffering from the disappearance of so many farm ponds and other watery sites in the countryside.

Go for variety

Not all of the visitors to your garden will be welcome guests, of course, but they will all add to the richness of the garden, and the great majority will do no harm. They are just using your garden as a home. The more habitats that you can create in your garden, the more guests you are likely to get, and the more diversity of wildlife. This can only be good for the wildlife population as a whole. If you find a strange creature in your garden, don't assume it is harmful. Find out what it is and does. You will probably find that it is harmless or even useful.

WILDLIFE-FRIENDLY GARDENS

Wildlife gardening involves creating an approximation to one or more natural habitats that will be acceptable to birds and other wild creatures. However, it does not mean giving the whole garden over to nature. You can continue to grow all your favourite flowers and vegetables in a wildlife garden.

The rough grass at the base of the wall in no way detracts from the appearance of this well-managed wildlife garden.

Useful guidelines

Although a large garden can obviously support more plant and animal life than a small one, size is not that important. Even a small garden can contain several wildlife habitats, such as a hedge, a small spinney or shrubbery, a pond and a grassy bank. It is what you plant in your garden that matters.

Cultivated varieties and exotic plants play a role in adding colour and excitement to a garden, but to be really wildlife friendly you need to grow a selection of native shrubs and other plants. These are the species on which our native insects have evolved, and if you provide food for the insects, then you will indirectly feed many of our garden birds as well.

Minimal gardening

Having created wildlife habitats for the insects and birds, you need to minimize any disturbance, so be less enthusiastic with the lawn mower and the hedge trimmer. Don't be tempted to dead-head all of your plants; this might encourage a longer flowering season but it does deprive birds and insects of food and shelter. Bare soil needs weeding, so cover your garden with as much vegetation as you can; this will keep down the weeds and give the birds a happy hunting ground. You might find that wildlife-friendly gardening is gardener-friendly as well!

Keep wildlife safe

Pick up any bottles and cans left in the garden after a party, or a well-earned drink. These containers can become coffins for small animals. Thousands of shrews and other small mammals die every year in carelessly abandoned bottles. Getting in to sample the dregs is easy, but climbing the smooth sides to get out again is not. Drink cans are not quite so bad, but beetles and many other useful creatures regularly drown in them.

FRUIT BUSHES AND NETTING

If you need to put nets over fruit bushes, make sure that they are taut and well anchored so that birds and other animals cannot get tangled up in them.

Great green bush-crickets are noisy inhabitants of many undisturbed garden hedges and shrubberies in southern England and on the European continent.

Let the brambles scramble over your hedge. Insects will sip nectar from the flowers in summer, and both you and the birds will be able to enjoy the fruits later in the year.

WEEDKILLERS AND PESTICIDES

If you cannot survive without using weedkillers or other pesticides, be sure to follow the instructions carefully, and dispose of any dregs where they cannot do any harm. It is very easy to kill vegetation and its associated animal life by the careless application of pesticides, especially in windy conditions when sprays can drift far from their intended targets.

Conservation tip

Do not use peat in your garden. Our peat bogs have shrunk alarmingly over the last 100 years or so because of the demand for peat from gardeners, and their wildlife has dwindled accordingly. Plenty of alternatives to peat are on the market now, and for hanging baskets there is 'Supermoss' – a sphagnum substitute which is made from recycled cloth and paper pulp.

A HEALTHY GARDEN

It took millions of years for nature to build up an equilibrium, in which each plant and animal species has its place and each helps to keep the rest under control. Nothing lives alone in nature; every creature either eats or is eaten by one or more other creatures. We have destroyed much of this delicate balance, but it is still not too late to put the process into reverse.

RESTORING THE BALANCE

The key thing is to live and work with nature, steering it in the direction we want in our gardens instead of destroying it. If we can achieve an approximation to nature's balance of predators and prey, then no one species will be able to multiply to such an extent that it becomes a nuisance. By creating natural habitats in your garden you will attract their characteristic wildlife. Trees and shrubs attract birds; ponds are magnets for frogs and toads; and flower beds pull in colourful insects. These guests will add considerable interest to your garden and will also do much to keep down the less desirable visitors – the pests. They will not eradicate the pests, but the amount of damage is likely to be minimal and you will be able to boast a healthy garden with a balanced ecology.

A typical garden food web

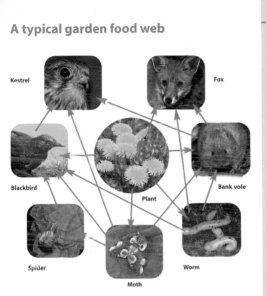

Kestrel

Fox

Blackbird

Bank vole

Plant

Spider

Worm

Moth

Moth feeds on nectar; spider eats moth; blackbird eats spider. This is a typical food chain. Many chains exist in a garden, and these are linked in a web – as most animals eat more than one kind of food. A few of the chains in a garden food web are illustrated here, with the arrows pointing from the food to the consumers. Each chain starts with a plant. With each species kept in check by its predators and/or food supplies, the whole community stays in a healthy equilibrium.

GARDEN FRIENDS AND FOES

Older nature books commonly listed the gardener's friends and foes, but now we know a lot more about the life histories of animals and how everything has its place in nature's complex web, it is not so easy to pigeon-hole them in this way. Nevertheless, we can identify some positively useful creatures (friends) that should be welcomed into the garden and some that our gardens would be better off without. These are the pests that eat our crops and spread diseases.

Lacewings often come to lighted windows at night. Why not try to introduce them to your roses or other plants where they can eat the troublesome aphids?

Friend or foe?
This simple, although not infallible, rule of thumb may help you to decide which are the goodies and which are the not-so-good. Fast-moving garden creatures are generally predators and on your side, whereas most slow-moving creatures tend to be herbivores and are thus often harmful in the garden.

Always a good and popular friend in our gardens, this hedgehog is busily polishing off a snail.

Our friends

Ground beetles These lurk under logs and stones, destroying slugs and many harmful caterpillars.

Lacewings These voracious carnivores destroy hundreds or even thousands of greenfly during their lives.

Hedgehogs These get rid of slugs and snails, though they do destroy the useful earthworms as well.

Ladybirds These little beetles eat huge numbers of greenfly and other harmful aphids.

Centipedes These eat slugs, insect grubs and other centipedes, which they kill with powerful venom.

Our foes

Lily beetles These bright red beetles destroy the leaves and seed capsules of all kinds of lilies. What look like slimy black droppings on the plants are actually the lily beetle grubs which are covered with their own excrement.

Aphids These tiny bugs occur in huge numbers and they deform many plants by sucking out the sap. They spread numerous viruses which are responsible for diseases such as potato leaf roll and various mosaics. There are hundreds of species.

Leatherjackets These rather featureless grey creatures are the grubs of crane-flies or daddy-long-legs. They live in the soil, especially under lawns and flower beds, and destroy the roots.

This apple shoot is deformed by the piercing beaks of sap-sucking aphids.

Cabbage white caterpillars Living in large clusters, the black and yellow caterpillars of the large white butterfly can quickly reduce a cabbage leaf to just a skeleton, and they give the cabbage a nasty smell.

Slugs Perhaps the most hated of all our garden residents, slugs nibble their way through flowers and vegetables. But not all slugs are pests: some of them prefer rotting leaves and fungi (see page 68).

Caterpillars of the large white butterfly here surround a solitary caterpillar of the small white. Both of these species are major pests of cabbages and other brassicas.

One of the worst of the gardener's foes: the netted slug is the one that we usually find in our lettuces.

PEST CONTROL

Gardening will always be a competition, with the gardener pitting his or her wits against an assortment of uninvited guests which are doing their best to damage the plants. Although you may have to get tough occasionally, it need not be all-out war. Live and let live is always a good motto for the gardener.

Avoid chemicals

You can buy chemicals, i.e. poisons, to control almost every garden visitor, but they have many drawbacks. There is a risk of killing useful or harmless creatures as well as pests. Killing useful creatures, e.g. ladybirds, may lead to an increase in the garden's aphid population and a tendency to use ever-increasing doses of insecticide. Although most modern pesticides break down rapidly in the soil, heavy applications may lead eventually to a build-up of residues that can damage the soil and enter the food chains, where they can have far-reaching and surprising effects.

Knock-on effects

Killing harmless creatures does have a knock-on effect by denying the birds and other animals their natural food, so your garden will be much less interesting. The true wildlife gardener uses non-poisonous means to discourage or get rid of pests.

Aphids, for example, can usually be controlled simply by squashing them with your fingers.

Re-cycling the empties – this lacewing larva, pictured here with its jaws plunged into an aphid, camouflages itself by piling the empty skins of its victims on its back.

Cultural control

Adjusting the way you grow things, or even what you grow, can make your garden less attractive to pests. Weeds can be eliminated with a layer of chipped bark or compost spread over the garden. Plant onions and carrots close together so the smell of the carrots deters or confuses the damaging onion-fly, and the smell of the onions discourages the carrot-fly. Roses or other flowers planted at the ends of vegetable rows attract hover-flies, which may lay their eggs on aphid-infested crops. Doing nothing and allowing nature's web to keep the pests in check is probably best of all. Losing a few plants to beetles and caterpillars is a price worth paying for a garden teeming with wildlife and no risk of poisoning yourself and your family.

Rose bushes are often planted in vineyards. Hover-flies are attracted to the flowers and lay their eggs on the vines, where their grubs attack aphids and other pests.

A song thrush with a snail in its beak. You can put out some bricks and large stones for them to use as anvils.

Biological control

This uses natural enemies to keep pests in check. Introducing ladybirds and their larvae to your garden can wipe out an infestation of aphids in days. Green lacewings do a good job on summer populations of aphids, and are useful in greenhouses throughout the year. Biological control of slugs can be achieved by using minute parasitic worms called *Plasmarhabditis hermaphrodita*. They seek out slugs and bore their way in. They multiply rapidly and the slugs explode, releasing another generation of worms. Snails can be kept in check by song thrushes if you have sufficient anvils on which the birds can break the shells. If you have no concrete paths or rockery stones, lay a few bricks or large stones around the garden.

PLANNING YOUR GARDEN

A wilderness and a wildlife garden are not the same! A wilderness does not exhibit the variety at the heart of a wildlife garden. It may have advantages for birds and hedgehogs, but, if left untouched, it will succumb to the processes of natural succession and turn into woodland in 20 years or so. If you want a wilderness, restrict it to a particular area and be prepared to tame it occasionally. Plan the rest of your wildlife garden carefully to make the best use of the available space.

A wildlife garden cannot be ideal for everything; it has to be a compromise. However, by growing lots of different plants you can create wonderful wildlife homes and still have room for your favourite flowers and vegetables – even in a small garden.

PLAN IT ON PAPER

Decide what features you want to include, which usually means what you have room for. Measure your garden so you can draw an accurate scale plan. Your aim is to have the flower beds and formal or tidier parts of your garden near to the house and let them grade into the wilder-looking areas further away. This gives the whole garden a natural look but allows you to control its structure. The pond should be in an open spot and bird tables should be positioned where you can see them.

When you have decided where everything is to go, think about the plants. The soil will influence what you can grow, so find out which plants do well in the area and which local flora are worth planting. Native species are best, but you don't have to ignore exotic species altogether. They lend superb colour and can provide just as much shelter for wildlife as our native species. Many also provide seasonal nectar and fruit.

A planned garden does not have to be formal. The position of this pond was actually carefully planned, but the plantlife gives it a wonderfully wild and natural appearance.

Hedges

Woodland margins are among the richest of all wild habitats, and an excellent way to reproduce them in your garden is to plant a hedge with a wavy margin, preferably on the northern or eastern boundary, or both, as this will help provide protection from cold winds without casting too much shade. A hedge will also enable you to grow primroses, foxgloves and many other sun-loving flowers at the base. Include as many different shrubs as possible to increase the hedge's attractiveness to birds and insects. Ideally, the hedge should be on your northern boundary, but shelter for you might mean shade for your neighbours.

Trees

A 'mini-spinney', with three or four small trees, is yet another excellent way to mimic the woodland edge. Birch is a good tree in such a situation because it does not cast deep shade. It also supports over 200 insect species in Britain, and several small birds enjoy its seeds in the autumn. Alder and hawthorn are nearly as effective in this respect. Rowan, bird cherry, hazel and crab apple are other good trees for this situation. Alternatively, you could try planting a cultivated apple; even a good cooker can support plenty of wildlife, from tiny insects to collared doves, and you can also enjoy the fruit yourself.

Among the most beautiful spring flowers, primroses grace many garden hedgerows. Look out for furry bee-flies plumbing the flowers for nectar with their long tongues.

Garden paths

These can be made of brick or concrete, or paving slabs laid as stepping stones across a lawn or through the flower beds. For a more natural look, however, lay some chipped bark over a firmly-rolled base, retained by a kerb of rustic poles. You can disguise the edge by planting violets and bugle and allowing them to tumble over the poles. Some interesting fungi may spring up on the poles and chippings. Try to make the paths curve through the garden so that you get new views at every turn and possibly a feeling that you are in a larger area. However, if you cannot do this, you can create an illusion of distance on a straight path by using large chips near the house and smaller ones further away. If your path is on a slope, put in some wooden steps here and there. Old railway sleepers are ideal, and if you drill a few holes in them you will probably attract various solitary bees (see page 175). You can also drill holes for them in the path edging.

Pergolas

Although pergolas tend to be associated with formal gardens, they can be wonderful wildlife centres. Clothed with roses or honeysuckle in summer, they attract insects and insect-eating birds, some of which nest in the dense climbers. You can make pergolas work for you in the winter by hanging different bird feeders on them. The sturdy uprights also make good supports for nest-boxes, but it is as well to move the feeders to another site before the

Bugle will make a colourful edging to a garden path in the spring. The wild form and various cultivars will be equally attractive to the bees.

nesting season begins: hordes of birds squabbling over a nearby bag of peanuts are not likely to make your nest-boxes desirable residences. Solitary bees and wasps will also appreciate your pergola if you drill a few small holes in the woodwork.

Pergolas that are allowed to become overgrown with an assortment of creepers can be superb for garden birds.

A WILDLIFE MEADOW

In the middle of the twentieth century, flower-rich meadows could be found in many parts of Britain, but less than two per cent survive today. Unfortunately, we cannot put them back, but every little helps and a flowery lawn in your garden is a good start.

Creating a flower-rich habitat

Scattering some native seeds on an existing lawn will not achieve very much because the grasses will swamp the seedlings, although you can increase their chances by removing the turf from small areas before sowing. The best approach is to strip all the turf and much of the top-soil away and then to re-seed the ground with a mixture of grass and flower seeds. The grass mixture should not include rye grass, which is too vigorous for a wildflower meadow.

GUIDELINES

Do not be tempted to sow too many species in a new lawn: four or five grasses and half a dozen flower species are plenty. Spread the grass seeds evenly over the area, but for a natural appearance the flower seeds should be sown in drifts of just two or three species. Never add any fertilizer to your meadow – this will merely encourage the grasses to grow and overshadow the other plants.

Abandon your mower and you will soon acquire a grassland jungle similar to this, where field mouse-ear and bird's foot trefoil are flowering below the thistles and tall flowerheads of the grasses

Choose your species

What you can grow successfully depends on the soil. Look at the surrounding countryside, including the roadside verges. Flowers that grow well there will do well in your meadow. Collect seeds by shaking the ripe seed-heads into paper bags, never dig up the plants.

It is very important to use native seeds; foreign seeds, even if they are the same species, may be adapted to different conditions and their genes may contaminate and damage our native flora. Sow your seeds in the autumn, but do not expect a mass of colour in the first summer – many seeds will not even germinate until the spring, and the young plants need a full season's growth before they are ready to flower.

Management is vital

Meadows were originally created by grazing and/or cutting, so you need to cut your flower meadow at least once a year. Use a scythe or a strimmer, but if you must use a mower don't set the blades too low.

- Cut in late summer or autumn for a good display of spring flowers, such as cuckoo flower, cowslip, fritillary, bugle and dandelion.
- Cut in spring and autumn for summer colour from the likes of knapweed, lady's bedstraw, scabious, meadow cranesbill and ox-eye daisy.

Drifts of delicate pink cuckoo flowers sometimes adorn many areas of damp grassland in the spring, and they are often accompanied by bright yellow cowslips.

MEADOW TIPS

Leave the cut vegetation on the ground for a day or two to allow any seeds to fall, but then clear it all away because a good flower meadow depends on poor soil fertility. If you have a large meadow area, you can mow some paths through it more frequently so that you can enjoy the flowers at close quarters.

Meadow plants
- Bladder campion
- Cowslip
- Cuckoo flower*
- Field scabious
- Greater knapweed
- Ox-eye daisy
- Meadow cranesbill
- Ragged robin*
- Self heal
- Yarrow

Plants marked * will thrive in damp areas.

NEAT EDGES

An area of long grass can look untidy even if it is full of flowers, so it is a good plan to mow the edge to stop grass tumbling on to your path or drive. You can mow the area nearest to the house as well and allow it to merge gradually into the longer grass, much as a golf course fairway grades into the rough.

HA-HA DITCH

If you live in open countryside, construct a ha-ha boundary (a sunken fence or ditch) so that your wild meadow appears to drift off into surrounding fields.

THE GARDEN HEDGE

Most houses have a boundary feature: a hedge or wall if you are lucky, but more often a wooden fence. Walls and fences can support a limited range of plant and animal life, but a mature hedgerow is a thriving community, teeming with insects and other animals while protecting your garden from the wind.

You could enrich your garden by replacing your fence with a hedge, or you could plant a low hedge inside

The attractive cultivated *Prunus* shrubs which make up this colourful flowering hedge are just as good a habitat for nesting birds as the wild shrubs.

Although it is extremely conspicuous when viewed on a bare twig, the 10 cm (4 in) caterpillar of the privet hawkmoth is surprisingly hard to spot in a privet hedge.

your boundary or even install one as the garden equivalent of a room-divider – separating your vegetable plot from your flower beds perhaps. Hedges are very cheap to create, although they do need more maintenance than walls and fences.

What to plant

Although the exotic plant species may bear plenty of tasty berries for the birds, they do not support many insects (see page 13), so our native shrubs are usually best for planting in a hedge.

Hawthorn is good as it grows quickly, even from cuttings, and is eaten by more than 150 insect species in Britain alone. Blackthorn, field maple, spindle, alder buckthorn, dogwood, buckthorn and guelder rose are also good. You can encourage honeysuckle, brambles and wild roses to scramble over the hedge. In fact, the more species you can incorporate, the better.

The animal residents

You would be surprised at how many animals live in a garden hedge. Here are some common residents.

BIRDS

Song thrushes, blackbirds, greenfinches, dunnocks and long-tailed tits all nest in garden hedges. The last two are happy to nest among slender twigs, but the others like to build in a stout fork and are most likely to nest in older hedges. Many more birds find food among the branches.

A hedgehog's spiky armour is formed from modified hairs. Although it is effective against most predators, it makes grooming difficult and hedgehogs usually carry fleas!

Garden project: planting a wildlife hedge
A hedge is best planted in the winter, and all the plants
should be pruned to no more than about 30 cm (12 in) in
height to encourage the growth of interlocking shoots.
A wildlife hedge does need trimming from time to time,
but only once every two years. By doing this, you will
always have some one-year-old wood on which many
of the shrubs carry their flowers. Trim half the hedge
one winter and the other half the next. Do keep it
narrower at the top than the bottom, or the ground
flora may become shaded out and some of the lower
branches may die back and leave gaps.

MAMMALS
Hedgehogs, shrews, mice and voles all forage in the
leaf litter at the base of hedges. Stoats and weasels –
Europe's smallest carnivores – may also hunt there.

INSECTS
These abound in hedgerows and they play a vital role
in feeding the local bird population. Look out for the
twig-like caterpillars of the swallowtailed moth and
some thorn moths. The hairy, colourful caterpillars
of the vapourer, grey dagger and yellowtail moths
are easier to find. Most birds avoid them because
the hairs of some species can cause severe irritation.
Spiders thrive on the insect life and their webs are
especially visible in the autumn.

WILDLIFE WALLS

Although hedges are always preferable as homes for wildlife, there is still a place for a wall in a wildlife garden, especially if it is located on some sloping ground, where small walls, no more than a metre (three feet) or so high, can be used to create a very attractive terraced effect.

This section of a dry stone wall shows the large through stones which are used to tie the two faces of the wall together. The central cavity can be filled with soil or small stones.

Conservation tip
Never be tempted to buy water-worn limestone, often sold as Westmorland stone. It should not be for sale anyway, as it comes from one of our rarest habitats – the much-damaged limestone pavements of northern Britain – which are now protected by law.

You don't need to be an expert bricklayer; in fact, you don't really need bricks at all. You can try building a dry stone wall, using one of the many traditional styles that are found in upland Britain. Always use local stone if possible, as this fits into the landscape so much better than alien material. You may be able to buy large stones from a local quarry or a nearby garden centre. Failing this, get hold of a copy of *The Natural Stone Directory* which will tell you where you can buy almost every kind of stone.

Red valerian is an attractive, although rather invasive, inhabitant of old walls. It attracts lots of butterflies and moths.

A wildlife refuge

Because there is no mortar between the stones, except perhaps at the ends of the wall, a dry stone wall offers homes to a huge variety of animals – lizards bask and hunt on the wall by day, while toads hide in the cool recesses along with numerous spiders and beetles.

Bumblebees will also take up residence, and in the warmer parts of Europe they may be joined by the harmless little scorpion *Euscorpius flavicaudis*. Wrens, black redstarts, great tits and pied wagtails are among the many birds that may find your wall to their liking. The hedgehog is sure to find a snug retreat among the lower stones. And don't forget yourself either: it is not difficult to incorporate a smooth stone slab in the wall so that you can sit comfortably and watch your garden guests.

The scorpion
Euscorpius flavicaudis
inhabits old walls in
southern Europe.
You may see the
pincers sticking out
of a crevice.

Garden project: building a dry stone wall

If your garden is flat, you can use low stone walls as decorative features or to create raised beds. These are ideal for alpines and many other plants and, once built, they make gardening much easier as well! Old bricks can be used instead of stone, but you still do not need mortar. Dig out the wall base to a depth of one brick, making sure that it is fairly level and compacted down.

To retain a bed, the wall should be double thickness and no higher than four courses. Set each course of bricks on a mixture of sand and peat-free compost. Leave a few gaps between the bricks for lizards and other small creatures to get in, but otherwise the bricks in each course need to be in contact with each other.

You won't have to wait long for ferns and other plants to spring up naturally in the sand/compost mixture and bind the bricks firmly together, but you can speed things up by planting some yourself. Houseleeks and stonecrops do very well on these walls.

Water your wall with a slurry of either cow or horse dung after building it to encourage invasion by various mosses and lichens, which will then act as nurseries for ferns and other plants. The wall will soon become a home for wildlife. Remember that this wall is not for walking or climbing on!

THE GARDEN POND

If you are really lucky your garden might already have a stream that you can dam to make a small pond. Local rocks can be used to form the dam, or you can utilize a tree trunk. Oak and elm are good for this as both timbers survive well under water.

Surrounded by a rich variety of wild and cultivated marginal plants, including yellow irises and brilliant orange primulas, this pond will attract a wide range of insects and other wildlife, and there is enough open water to encourage frogs and dragonflies to come and lay their eggs.

A height of 50 cm (20 in) is fine for the dam. Consult the appropriate authorities if you want to create a larger pool because anything more than a small dam could interfere with water supplies further downstream.

Most of us will have to create our ponds from scratch, but this is not difficult if there are strong people to do the digging. Pond plants and animals like plenty of sunshine, so don't site your pond under trees. Apart from creating shade, they will drop their leaves into the water in the autumn and cause a lot of problems. If you compare a woodland pool with one in the open, you will be in no doubt that the latter is a much richer and more attractive habitat.

CONSTRUCTING THE POND

Ponds dug in low-lying areas where the water table is close to the surface sometimes fill themselves, and you can't ask for much more natural ponds than these. Otherwise you will have to line your pond.

PREFORMED FIBREGLASS LINER

If you decide on a preformed fibreglass liner, all you have to do is to buy one of the shape and size that you want, dig a similarly shaped hole, and drop the liner into it (see overleaf). A morning's work can give you a very attractive pond!

1 Mark the position of the pond with some pegs and string or a line of sand for irregular shapes.

2 The excavation must match the profile of the unit. Measure all depths carefully from the rim.

3 Allow for installation of the pool and back-filling by digging out a larger hole than marked.

4 After removing all the stones, you should make sure that the ground is compacted down.

5 Smooth the sides and spread a 5 cm (2 in) protective layer of sand on the base and sides.

6 Press the unit gently until level, and then part-fill with water and back-fill with some sifted soil or sand.

This shows the correct level for a shelf for marginal plants. The surrounding paving stones must be cemented into place and overhang the edge sufficiently to conceal the edges of the liner. Frogs may shelter under these overhangs, but you need to provide one or more stepping stones so that the animals can get out of the pond.

FLEXIBLE LINERS

These allow you to have virtually any shaped pond. You can use heavy-duty black polythene, but butyl rubber is better and lasts longer. Whatever you get, ensure it has at least a 10-year guarantee. Calculate the required liner size by measuring the maximum length and breadth of the pond, adding twice the maximum depth to each dimension, and then adding 50 cm (20 in) to each to allow for sufficient overlap at the margins. You can choose any shape but butyl rubber liners are usually rectangular, so long, narrow ponds tend to be rather wasteful of this lining material.

1 Mark out the shape of the pond with either a rope or a hose-pipe before you begin digging. Make the pond as big as you can.

2 Make sure the edges are level. The central area should be at least 50 cm (20 in) deep so the whole pond does not freeze solid in a hard winter.

3 Start digging in the centre. Slope the bottom up gently with a shelf 13 cm (6 in) below the surface on one side.

4 Line the hole with soft sand and spread the liner over it. Weight the edges down and start adding water.

5 When the pond is full, tidy up the margins. You can hide the liner edges under some concrete, stone slabs, turf or large pebbles.

6 Leave everything to settle for a few days. When you are happy that the margins are level and properly covered, start planting your pond.

CLEANING AND MAINTENANCE

Well-sited ponds with a good balance of plants and animals should not need much maintenance, but most garden ponds do need attention from time to time. Rotting leaves use up oxygen, causing the bottom of the pond to become black and smelly, so remove any dead vegetation in the autumn before frogs start to settle down in the mud for the winter. Leave the material on the side for a day or two so that any animals in it can find their way back to the water.

This moorhen's nest has been built on a small rocky island in the middle of a pond. The bird is about to sit on the eggs, which the other parent has just left.

Green water

Green algae often turn pond water green in the summer. Although this is not harmful, it does make pond-watching more difficult. The problem is most common in ponds that do not have a good growth of submerged plants to use up the nutrients. Green water problems can also occur when ponds are filled with tap water, because the high mineral content of the water encourages algae to multiply rapidly.

Several ecologically friendly products are available to combat the problem, but first you could try adding a bundle of barley straw to your pond. As the straw breaks down, it releases substances that appear to kill the algae. You can get the straw at most good aquatic centres, together with information on the quantities needed.

Which water source?

The tap is usually the only source of water for the pond but, as explained above, tap water can cause green water problems. The best thing of all, if you are planning to have a pond in your garden, is to store up a supply of rain water ready for filling it.

Always use rain water to top up your pond in the summer: an adaptor fitted to a drainpipe can be used to divert water into a hose leading to the pond.

MARSH GARDENS

Many natural ponds are surrounded by marshy areas, and it is quite easy to create this habitat around your garden pond when you are constructing it.

Creating a marsh garden

If you're using a flexible liner, dig a shallow extension, 20–25 cm (8–10 in) deep, at one end or side of the pond. Leave a ridge, a few centimetres below the final water level, between the two excavations. Spread the liner over it and into the shallow marsh area.

A mixture of wild and cultivated flowers can produce a riot of colour in a marsh garden.

Edge with turf or stone. Create a barrier between the pond and the extension with a large oak or elm log laid on the ridge or a couple of courses of bricks (without mortar) topped by turf or stone slabs.

Mix the excavated soil with some good compost, but do ensure that it is free from sharp stones, and then return it to the incipient marsh. When you fill the pond, water will seep into the marsh, but the barrier should stop the soil running into the pond. Remember to leave a certain amount of firm ground on the edge where you can stand or sit to watch the pond life.

Mud-loving plants

Marsh marigolds, purple loosestrife, yellow iris, bogbean, ragged robin and water mint will all grow happily in the waterlogged soil of your marsh and will attract lots of insects. Frogs and toads will enjoy the food and shelter in this watery habitat, and they will control the slugs in other parts of your garden.

Safety tip
Ponds and young children do not mix well, so if you have youngsters stick to a marsh, or fence your pond with green wire fencing. A fence about half a metre high will keep out toddlers, as well as most dogs, and can be hidden in the vegetation around the pond.

STOCKING YOUR POND

A natural pond will normally have three ecological groups of plants: submerged, floating and emergent. Try to include representatives of all three groups.

Submerged species

These may thrust their flowers above the surface but they will remain underwater for the most part, providing the pond with much of its oxygen.

A rich mixture of marginal and floating plants gives this pond a balanced and natural appearance. The nearby trees are far enough away not to cast heavy shade on the water.

Hornwort, Canadian waterweed and water milfoil are among the best of these oxygenators. Throw a few pieces into your pond and they will quickly produce dense clumps of vegetation. Water violet is also worth growing for its spikes of violet-coloured flowers.

Floating plants

Best known of the floating plants are, of course, the water lilies. You can grow cultivated forms as well as our native yellow and white species; they all provide nectar for insects, and their leaves will make good perches for dragonflies and frogs. Water lilies are best grown in the deepest part of the pond, planted in plastic baskets that are weighted down with stones. The fringed water lily, a member of the bogbean family, is a much more delicate plant, worth trying in the shallower parts of the pond, together with amphibious bistort. Both produce attractive flowers.

DUCKWEED

The smallest of all the flowering plants, duckweed will arrive in your pond sooner or later. Small patches can be quite attractive, but don't let it cover the surface and cut off the light from the submerged plants. Do keep all your floating plants in check, and ideally try to keep about half of the surface area free of any vegetation so that it will attract dragonflies and other aquatic insects (see page 178).

Emergent plants

These provide nectar for visiting insects and essential cover for amphibians and other creatures moving in and out of the water. Early on summer mornings you may well see dragonfly nymphs crawling up them in readiness for the dramatic change to the adult stage.

Good emergent plants for your pond include the following: flowering rush, arrowhead, bogbean, water mint, brooklime, water forget-me-not, lesser spearwort, yellow iris and purple loosestrife.

Put marginal plants, e.g. arrowhead, in plastic baskets on shelves

Free-floating plants, e.g. water soldier and frogbit, float on the surface

Floating-leaved plants, e.g. water lilies and pondweed in baskets on bricks adjusted for depth

Pond liner

Submerged plants (oxygenators), e.g. water milfoil, are rooted in baskets on the bottom

Offcut of underlay protects liner from edges of bricks

Bogbean

Flowering rush

PLANTING AND BUYING EMERGENT PLANTS

These are all best planted in baskets on the marginal shelf or in the shallows. They can be obtained from most good garden or aquatic centres, or can be scrounged from other pond owners. However, you should never take them from the wild.

Log or large stones fixed to retain soil

Moisture-loving marsh plants, e.g. water plantain, in waterlogged soil at edge

Floating-leaved and submerged plants rooted in soil on bottom

This shows how a pond and marginal marsh can be made with a flexible liner, and demonstrates how submerged and marginal plants can be planted.

POND-DWELLERS

These fall into three ecological groups: free-swimming creatures, including beetles and bugs, fishes and small crustaceans; the crawlers, such as worms and snails and a variety of young insects; and the surface-dwelling pond skaters and whirligig beetles. The water surface behaves as if it has a thin skin, and if you look carefully at the pond skaters you will see the little dimples made by their water-repellent feet.

Attracting animals to the pond

Most animals will find their way to your pond by themselves, but you can 'seed' a new pond with a few bucketfuls of water taken from an existing pond or a water butt. This introduces some of the microscopic organisms on which most other pond life depends.

Newts live partly in the water and partly on land, but they tend to be more aquatic than frogs and toads.

Pond skaters skim rapidly over the pond surface on their long, water-repellent legs in search of other insects that fall into the water.

Diving beetles, pond skaters, water boatmen, mayflies, dragonflies and mosquitoes will not take long to arrive. Frogs and newts quickly discover new ponds, but toads are less likely to arrive under their own steam because they normally return to the ponds where they grew up. Scrounge a bit of spawn or some tadpoles from a neighbour's pond if you want to have some toads. But avoid the temptation to put fish in anything but a large pond because they will eat many of the other animals!

Pond snails can be useful for controlling green algae, but if you have too many in your pond, they may eat the plants as well

A LOG GARDEN

The woodland floor is a surprisingly rich habitat where fungi and a host of small animals break down and recycle the dead wood and leaves. Without these vital organisms, the human race would have been buried under a mountain of dead wood long ago: in fact, we would probably never have evolved.

CREATING A LOG GARDEN

It is easy to create a replica of the woodland floor in a shady corner of your garden. Stack up a few logs with plenty of gaps between them; surround the stack with a bed of wood or bark chippings.

Which logs?

Use logs of varying thicknesses, and try to get wood of several different species, such as oak, beech, ash, elm and pine. This will increase the variety of insects and other creatures, and you can watch the gradual disintegration of the timber over several years as a succession of fungi and other organisms move in.

Mosses, lichens and fungi

Mosses and lichens may already be growing on the bark when you get the logs. Although they don't do

When building a log garden, don't forget to leave a few gaps for the mice and hedgehogs to get in. Solitary bees and wasps may tunnel into the softer logs.

much towards breaking down the timber, they act as nurseries for ferns and other plants whose roots get under the bark and open the way for animal life. The toadstools and bracket fungi that may sprout from the logs are the reproductive parts that scatter the spores. Most of the fungus consists of hair-like threads which spread through the timber and soften it.

Toadstools most often appear on logs in the autumn. A cluster like this can scatter millions of spores, but very few will reach a suitable spot in which to grow.

Maintenance

Add fresh logs and wood chips occasionally so you always have timber in various stages of decay. The completely rotted material can be spread on your garden. Spray the logs with water in dry weather, as the resident plants and animals don't like to get too dry.

Wildlife inhabitants

Dead wood in the forest is the natural home of the furniture beetle (woodworm) and other timber pests, and these insects are among the first to attack your logs. As the timber softens, they may be followed by stag beetles and the much more common lesser stag beetles, whose fat, juicy grubs tunnel through the timber for several years.

Endomychus coccineus is a ladybird look-alike that feeds on fungal threads under the bark. Woodlice and millipedes live under loose bark and will eat the timber softened by the fungi. Centipedes, spiders

> **Conservation tip**
> Do not construct your log garden too close to any old or valuable trees. Honey fungus may well invade the logs and it could spread to living trees. Although young, healthy trees are rarely harmed, older specimens are sometimes killed by the fungus.

The antlers of the male stag beetle (right) are much enlarged jaws, and they are used to fight over the females. The latter have much smaller jaws and look more like the lesser stag beetle (below right), although they are not as black.

and ground beetles hunt in and around the logs, and many other invertebrates find food and shelter there. Don't be afraid to lift one of the logs occasionally to see what is lurking underneath.

Wrens love to hunt insects and spiders in the log garden, while hedgehogs, mice and voles often make their homes there. Little piles of grain and other fruits or seeds hidden are signs that they are in residence.

HEALTHY SOIL

With a wildlife population ranging from microscopic bacteria, through worms and other creepy-crawlies to moles, your soil is a living community.

INDISPENSABLE EARTHWORMS

Charles Darwin reckoned the earthworm to be the most important animal in the history of the world. A 1000 m^2 plot of good garden loam may support 25,000 worms which, by pushing and chewing their way through the soil, can create up to 5 km (3 miles) of new tunnels each day! Although the tunnels may not last very long, they play a major role in draining and aerating the soil – and Darwin realized this is vital for the well-being of plant roots.

Centipedes are often called 'wireworms'. Numerous joints enable them to bend their bodies in any direction.

Half in and half out of their burrows, these earthworms snuggle up and dig their bristles into each other before they exchange sperm. Earthworms are hermaphrodite with both male and female organs in each individual.

Enriching the soil

Worms enrich the soil by dragging dead leaves into it and bringing mineral-rich material up to the surface where it can be used by plant roots. Worm-casts help promote the growth of vitamin-secreting bacteria, and the vitamin improves root growth and crop yield.

Treating your flowers and vegetables to organic manure is far better for the worms than spraying them with chemical fertilizers. Worms feed on organic matter and you have only to look in your compost heap to see how well they flourish when they are surrounded by rotting vegetation.

THE COMPOST HEAP

Composting your organic rubbish not only converts your kitchen and garden waste into plant food but also helps the whole environment by reducing the amount of material going to land-fill sites.

What to compost

Any organic material can be composted, including dead leaves, grass cuttings, hedge clippings, weeds, potato peelings and tea bags. Build your heap on a layer of twigs to let air into the base. Bacteria will soon get to work on the material, producing heat that

The brandling worm, which is easily recognized by its bold rings, is the commonest earthworm in most compost heaps.

Cryptops is a blind but very active centipede with 21 pairs of legs. The last pair are very stout and act like extra antennae.

steps up the rate of decay. Surrounding the heap with wooden planks or corrugated iron sheets helps keep in the warmth, as does covering it with some carpet. The rate of conversion to compost depends on the temperature and type of material in the heap. You can speed it up by adding horse manure or a sprinkling of nitrogenous fertilizer to encourage bacterial growth.

Teeming with wildlife

A compost heap is also a happy hunting ground for numerous animals, many of whom play a major role in the breakdown and eventual decay of the material. Feeding on smaller creatures or rotting vegetation, they range from microscopic mites to hedgehogs.

The smaller animals are not evenly distributed through the compost. Brandling worms like the moister parts and abound in layers of grass clippings or dead leaves, whereas woodlice and some centipedes prefer slightly drier parts of the heap and scurry around when you disturb the material. Slugs and snails will wander all over the compost heap at night or after some rain, and it is also worth looking out for the extraordinary aerial courtship of the great grey or leopard slug. Up to 15 cm (6 in) long, the slugs meet in the compost and then, after a prolonged slimy embrace, they climb a fence post or other vertical surface. Tightly entwined, they then lower themselves on a rope of mucus and mating finally takes place in mid-air, often a metre or two above the ground and well out of the reach of marauding hedgehogs!

On returning to the ground, each slug goes off and lays its eggs. Slugs are hermaphrodite creatures with both male and female organs in each individual.

The pincers look threatening and usually carry a powerful venom, but the false scorpion is no more than 4 mm long.

THE SMALLEST WILDLIFE

If you want to see the smaller inhabitants of your compost heap, spread out a handful of compost on a white surface and examine it with a magnifying glass. Grotesque mites mingle with tiny beetles, while springtails leap into the air at the slightest disturbance. The droppings of all these tiny animals will make up a high proportion of the older and more decayed compost. The predatory false scorpions possess some of the animal kingdom's most potent venom but, luckily, are too small to hurt us. They usually arrive in the heap by hitching lifts on flies and other insects, to which they cling with their relatively huge pincers.

Woodlice are mainly nocturnal and tend to huddle together in damp places during the day. Two species are resting on this piece of wood lifted from a compost heap.

PART TWO

Garden mammals

Garden mammals are warm-blooded animals with fur coats. About 30 species might visit a rural garden but fewer are likely to take up permanent residence. Represented by herbivorous, carnivorous and omnivorous species, they range in size from tiny shrews and bats to deer. Most of them will come into your garden whether you like it or not, although you may not be aware of them because they are generally nocturnal and rather quiet. Apart from deer and squirrels, which can damage trees and shrubs, most of these visitors are pretty harmless. Hedgehogs do a lot of good by eating harmful slugs and other pests, so it is always worth encouraging them into your garden.

The grey squirrel

This common visitor to our gardens in both town and countryside is not always welcome despite its attractive appearance.

READING THE SIGNS

Most of our mammals are nocturnal so it is not easy to see them going about their business. However, they leave plenty of clues in the form of footprints, food remains and droppings, and with a little bit of detective work you can usually find out which ones visit your garden at night.

TELL-TALE SIGNS

One easy way to discover which animals explore your garden during the night is to put down a patch of damp, soft sand and then look for any footprints in it in the morning. You can encourage the animals to walk over the sand by leaving various foods in the middle. Some bread

A badger's footprint can be easily identified by its breadth and by the long, chunky impressions of its toes – usually five, although the inner toe does not always leave a mark.

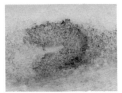

Footprints are easy to spot and follow in the snow, although they are usually less clear than those left on muddy ground. This is the print or slot of a roe deer, up to 5 cm (2 in) long.

which has been flavoured with aniseed is said to be especially attractive to mice and other small mammals. You can also try fruit, sliced carrot, grain and a portion of pet food. These should attract a variety of wildlife which will leave plenty of tracks for you to interpret. Even beetles and earwigs leave footprints if the ground is soft enough.

Another way to detect the presence of small mammals is to put some bait in the centre of a sheet of paper that has been smoked over a candle. Little feet pick up the smoke particles and leave clear tracks.

Hairy evidence

Larger mammals, including badgers and deer, often leave hairs behind them when they brush against thorny bushes or pass through or under wire fences. It is usually possible to identify the hairs. The long outer hairs of the badger, for example, are dark in the centre and pale at the base and the tip. Because these

animals tend to tread regular pathways, finding tufts
of hair will show you where to watch for them at night.

Observing mammals at night

If you can't see the spot from your house or garden
shed, then you can try rigging up a simple hide. An
old, dark curtain hung on a bamboo frame can be
quite effective if you cut small holes for your torch
and binoculars. The animals do not like bright lights
and you are less likely to alarm them if you cover your
torch with a piece of red plastic. Of course, image
intensifiers or infra-red binoculars are the ideal
equipment, but these are much too expensive for
most garden-watchers.

Pine cones that are
stripped like these
ones indicate that
squirrels have been
busy. Mice make
a much neater job
of removing the
cone scales.

How to crack a nut

Hazel nuts are eagerly sought by many mammals and each species has its own way of opening them. Look for the opened nuts under a hazel tree if you have one. Alternatively, scatter some nuts on the ground and wait for them to be opened – but don't be surprised if most of them are taken away for opening and eating. Nuthatches and woodpeckers, for example, wedge the nuts into bark crevices and hammer them open.

A squirrel splits a hazel nut cleanly in half by nibbling a little hole at the top and then using its lower front teeth to prise the two halves apart.

The bank vole gnaws a neat hole in the top or at the side of the nut, leaving an extremely clean edge on the outer surface of the nut.

The wood mouse gnaws a hole in the side of the nut but it always leaves a distinctive ring of tooth marks around the outside of the hole.

HEDGEHOGS

The prickly hedgehog is probably the most familiar and engaging of our nocturnal mammalian visitors. It is certainly the easiest one to watch as it trundles across the lawn in search of worms, beetles and other tasty morsels on a summer evening.

The hedgehog's eyesight is not brilliant and you can usually get quite close to it; you don't even need a red filter on your torch. The animal may roll into a spiky ball if you make sudden movements or sounds, but it is just as likely to sit quietly and stare back at you.

Hedgehog courtship, which can be witnessed through the summer, usually starts with the male trotting round and round the female and snorting loudly.

> **Conservation tip**
> If you find a baby hedgehog in the garden after the
> middle of September, try to catch it and stick it on your
> kitchen scales. If it weighs less than about 450 g (1 lb)
> it is unlikely to survive the winter in the wild, as it will
> not have enough fat on it. Take it in and feed it up,
> remembering to dust it with flea powder! Once it has
> reached 500 g (1 lb 2 oz) or so, you can release it or
> keep it indoors through the winter. It won't bother
> about hibernation if you keep it warm.

However, if you take your eyes off it for just a moment,
it will probably disappear without a sound – it is
remarkably quick for an animal with short legs.

On the other hand, the hedgehog can be extremely
noisy, especially when scratching for food in the hedge
bottom or the herbaceous border: it is not called the
hedgepig for nothing. Courtship is also a noisy and
very public affair, with much grunting and squealing
as the pair leap around each other on the lawn.

HEDGEHOG DINNERS

Hedgehogs will often eat birds' eggs and occasionally
catch mice, frogs and even snakes, but invertebrates
are their favourite food. Examination of their sausage-
shaped droppings will reveal a high proportion of

beetle remains. Caterpillars and earthworms are equally important, although they contain fewer indigestible remains. Garden hedgehogs will always appreciate some additional food, and a saucer of mealworms is likely to attract several animals. They are equally happy with a plate of dog food, garnished with some sliced apple or dried fruit.

Bread and milk has long been the traditional snack for hedgehogs but, although nourishing, it should not be given too often because, like us, hedgehogs need a balanced diet. Extra food is extremely valuable in dry summer weather when worms and other creepy-crawlies burrow down out of reach, and also in the autumn when the hedgehogs are preparing for their winter sleep. Giving them additional food at such times can save their lives.

WINTER QUARTERS

As the days shorten in the autumn, the hedgehogs fatten themselves up and search out some suitable sleeping quarters – often in a hedge bottom, a log pile or a compost heap. Each animal busies itself gathering dead leaves and then packing them into a recess to form a ball up to 50 cm (20 in) in diameter. The hedgehog then burrows into it and settles down for the winter.

If you are any good at sticking bits of wood together you can help your garden hedgehogs by making them a box with a hedgehog-sized opening. Fill it with leaves and shove it into your compost heap. Alternatively, simply cover it with branches – a good use for leylandii trimmings perhaps – and one of the local hedgehogs will be more than happy to move in. If you are no good at working with wood, you can buy hedgehog homes at garden centres and pet shops.

Garden hedgehogs will readily nest in boxes like this during the summer. Put the box in a secluded spot, half-fill it with leaves and then cover it with a sack or some branches. Do not use straw or hay as bedding as the sharp stems can cause injuries.

RODENTS

With about 1,700 species, the rodents are the largest
of all the groups of mammals. Characterized by their
continuously-growing, chisel-like front teeth that can
gnaw through almost anything, they include rats and
mice, voles, squirrels and beavers.

MICE

Although they are not the most welcome of garden
guests, because of their liking for newly-sown peas
and other vegetables, these little mammals can be
amusing to watch and, of course, they will attract a
number of equally fascinating predators, including
stoats, weasels and
kestrels. I doubt if
there is a garden
anywhere without a
few mice and voles,

Its large eyes and
huge ears indicate that
the wood mouse is
essentially a nocturnal
creature. It is hardly ever
seen during daylight.

but they rarely show themselves. If you want to watch them you will have to encourage them by putting out little piles of breakfast cereal or peanut butter. The woodmouse is the mouse most likely to be seen in the garden. Look for its bulging eyes and very large ears. It lives in hedgerows, compost heaps, woodpiles or under garden sheds. The house mouse has smaller eyes than the woodmouse and lacks the white belly. It normally stays close to houses and sheds.

VOLES

A vole has a shorter and blunter snout than a mouse and its tiny ears are almost hidden in its fur. The bank vole, which is identified by its reddish-brown fur, is common in many rural gardens, where it forages in hedge bottoms and shrubberies. It also climbs well and is not averse

The bank vole is active by day and night. It eats some worms and insects, but it is largely vegetarian and seeds are its main food.

to a meal of raspberries and some other soft fruits. The much duller field vole likes more open areas with long grass, including orchards. If you have room to lay down some corrugated sheets you might well find field voles nesting under them.

THE GARDEN DORMOUSE

Although absent from Britain, the garden dormouse is widely distributed through Western Europe and is one of the most attractive garden visitors. A little smaller than a rat, it is readily distinguished by the bushy black and white tip to its tail and the black 'mask' enclosing its eyes and the base of each ear. Easily lured with nuts and fruit, sometimes it will take up residence in boxes intended for birds.

It often gets into houses and makes a lot of noise when scampering around the loft at night. It can also produce considerable mess with its droppings and is not averse to hibernating in the spare room!

SQUIRRELS

These are the most obvious rodents in many gardens, especially those with trees. The red squirrel occurs on the European mainland, but the somewhat larger grey squirrel – introduced from North America – is

Grey squirrels quickly become tame in parks and gardens where they are fed regularly, but feeding these animals is not to be encouraged as they damage trees and plants!

the only one found in most parts of England and Wales. The animals quickly learn to take peanuts (unsalted) from your hand, and it is fun to watch them stripping pine and spruce cones to obtain the seeds, but they can be a nuisance at the bird table. Few of the so called squirrel-proof feeding devices defeat these intelligent creatures for long. As well as eating nuts and other seeds, they strip bark, eat fungi and dig up bulbs and corms; in the spring they eat birds' eggs and nestlings. So it is not a brilliant idea to encourage squirrels into your garden.

FOXES

You will know if a fox has wandered through your garden because everywhere it goes it leaves its characteristic smell, which resembles that of the weed herb robert. The best way to learn what reynard smells like is to go for a walk with someone who already knows the odour, or to a zoo or wildlife park and have a good sniff; then you will recognize the strong, musky scent when you encounter it.

ATTRACTING FOXES

Foxes are extremely common, even in towns. In fact, they are more widespread in many urban areas than they are in the countryside. They are real scavengers and obtain a lot of their food from dustbins. Although few people are prepared to encourage foxes into their gardens, it is very easy to attract them to a plate of dog food placed on the lawn at night (as long as the neighbourhood cats do not get there first).

Use red torchlight to watch from your window and, with a bit of luck, you will see what a handsome creature the fox is. It might scratch around for worms, but otherwise it will do no harm in your garden as long as you lock up your chickens and other livestock.

Foxes are essentially solitary creatures, but two or three may gather where food is put out regularly.

BADGERS

Although not many people can claim ever to have seen a badger, these heavily-built nocturnal creatures are really quite common wherever areas of deciduous woodland are interspersed with open country.

Badgers emerge from their sets in the evening and may cover several kilometres as they search out a variety of plant and animal food. They frequently visit railway embankments and cemeteries.

Although badgers live in communities, they usually forage by themselves. Like foxes, they will feed together if food is provided. Tempt them with fruit as well as meaty foods.

ATTRACTING BADGERS

If your garden is close to deciduous woodland the chances are that you will be able to attract badgers with a dish of dog food and some table scraps. If the food is put out regularly, any badgers that find it will soon include your garden in their nightly rounds and will become regular visitors.

Badgers are fond of earthworms and may pull your compost heap to pieces in search of them. Occasionally they dig up lawns in search of moles, but you can usually divert their attention with other food. It is exciting to see them materialize silently out of the twilight, and the enjoyment you get from watching them outweighs any damage they might do.

The bold black and white stripes on the head may help badgers to recognize each other at night, or may be a warning to other animals.

BATS

Most gardens, even those in the middle of towns, are visited by bats at night. You will often see them circling street lamps at high speed to snap up the moths and other insects that are drawn to the light.

Although we cannot actually hear them, bats continually emit high-frequency sounds, which are way above our hearing range, and they use the echoes to detect their insect prey. This echo-location system enables bats to navigate and avoid obstacles, so you need have no fear that they will bump into you.

All of our bats feed on insects and they fly only in the warmer months. They hibernate in the winter when there are not enough insects for them to eat.

Conservation tip

In the United Kingdom, bats and their roosts are fully protected by the Wildlife and Countryside Act and you must not do anything to harm them. If you have a problem with a roost in your house, contact your County Wildlife Trust or the Bat Conservation Trust to get advice on what you should do (see page 189). However, bats rarely cause problems, so just enjoy having these fascinating creatures as guests.

Although they use echo-location to navigate and find their food, the bats are not really blind, but you will have to look hard to spot the eyes of this pipistrelle bat.

SPECIES OF BAT

Of the 16 bat species to be found in Great Britain, only three of them are commonly seen over our gardens: the common pipistrelle, the much larger serotine and the brown long-eared bat. The common pipistrelle is the one that we normally see at night swooping around the garden at a height of 2–3 m (6–9 ft). It is also Britain's smallest bat, weighing in at no more than about 8 g (1/4 oz) although it has a wingspan of about 25 cm (10 in).

BAT HOMES

Most bats are associated with hollow trees, caves and old buildings, but their loss or 'improvement' has led to the decline of several species. The pipistrelle can find plenty of roosting sites, even in modern houses, but still appreciates additional accommodation.

A rough board or a couple of planks screwed to a pair of vertical battens provides a fine summer roosting place if fixed just under the eaves on a south- or west-facing house wall, and then you may be able to enjoy the sight of the bats at dusk streaming out to feed. Pipistrelles are sociable and 50 or more individuals may use such a roost.

Schwegler boxes make ideal homes for bats. Fix them to tree trunks in pairs, one on each side of the trunk, so the bats can move if they get too hot.

Wildlife project: bat roost
This is a simple wall-mounted bat roost. The slit opening at the bottom should be no more than 2 cm (3/4 in) wide. Fixed to a north-facing wall, it might be used as a winter roost. You must not treat the timber with any kind of wood preservative as most of these are poisonous to bats.

However, don't expect it to be occupied right away. Pipistrelles also have a touch of gypsy in them, so do not be surprised if they use the roost for a while and then move away. Find out if your roost is occupied by putting a plank of wood on the ground below: if bats are in residence you will find droppings on the wood.

Bat rescue

Baby bats start to fly at three or four weeks old but they are not very good initially and many of them fall to the ground below the roost. Unable to get airborne again, most perish, so it is worthwhile trying to return them to the roost. Alternatively, you can keep them warm indoors and feed them with skimmed milk and crushed mealworms until they are strong enough to fly. Release them at dusk.

PART THREE

Garden birds

All gardens have some bird life; even the barest town garden has a few house sparrows searching for crumbs. Robins, blue tits and many other common garden birds are with us all year round. We also get summer visitors from Africa, mostly insect-eaters like swallows, house martins and spotted flycatchers. Residents and summer visitors may nest in our gardens if we provide the right vegetation or nest boxes, although most of the birds we see are passing through. We also get winter visitors from northern Europe. Along with our resident birds, they will brighten any garden and will appreciate the food that we put out for them. Our gardens certainly would not be the same without them.

The great tit

Easily recognized by its black and white head and yellow front, the great tit is common in our gardens throughout the year and takes up residence in nest boxes.

A BEAK FOR THE JOB

Birds have evolved the ability to deal with virtually every kind of food on offer, from minute seeds and insects, through fruits of all kinds, to fish, flesh and carrion. Each bird's beak or bill is beautifully adapted for its diet and the chosen task. The members of each family usually have similar diets, and therefore similar beaks. Finch beaks range from the tiny tweezer-like apparatus of the goldfinch to the hawfinch's 'sledge-hammer', able to crack cherry stones. All these birds are seed-eaters but they avoid competing with each other by specializing in different kinds of seeds.

ON THE LEVEL

Blue tits and great tits eat the same kinds of food but forage at different levels – blue tits mainly in tree branches and great tits on or near the ground. If they did not divide up the food source in this way the great tit would slowly wipe out the smaller blue tit. Swallows and house martins also share out the available food by hunting at different levels – swallows usually feed within 30 m (90 ft) of the ground while house martins are most likely to be seen above 50 m (150 ft). Remember the different dietary preferences of birds when feeding them in the garden. Do not

Left: The chaffinch's beak is not highly specialized. It is stout and strong enough to crack many seeds, but at the same time dainty enough to be able to peck insects from bark crevices.

Right: The wren specializes in insects and spiders. Its slender beak can pick them up easily and has no trouble in crushing their soft bodies.

Left: Woodpeckers use their beaks like chisels to dig for insects in tree trunks, but the green woodpecker is more likely to feed on ants on the ground.

expect all your visitors to be content with bread crumbs and an occasional treat of peanuts. The greater the variety of food you provide, the larger your reward in terms of the number of bird species visiting your garden.

FOOD FOR THE BIRDS

Birds can usually find plenty to eat by foraging, but you can make life easier for them by providing extra food. They will soon get to know when and where to expect their meals, and their meal-time antics will be ample reward for a modest outlay on food.

THE BIRD TABLE

Many birds are happy to pick up the food you scatter on the ground. Indeed, blackbirds and dunnocks prefer to take their meals on the ground, but where

A roof may deter some birds, but not these starlings, which often arrive in gangs and chase the smaller birds away.

most species are concerned a table will benefit both the birds and bird-watcher. The table need not be elaborate: a simple tray about 50 cm (20 in) square and equipped with a rim and a few drainage holes is perfectly adequate. A roof is certainly not necessary

Siting the table

Ideally the table should be fixed to the top of a smooth metal pole about 2 m (6 ft) high. Place it out of reach of any predatory cats and make it safe from squirrels. If you have no secure spot for a pole-mounted table, you could fix one to a wall. Hanging one from a rope tied to two trees will keep it safe from cats, but not squirrels. The table should be no more than 2 m (6 ft) from cover, so that the birds can dart for safety if a sparrowhawk or another danger appears.

You need to be able to see the table clearly from a window, so don't site it where it will be in deep shade. The north side of the house is best, as the birds will not be silhouetted against the sun for much of the day. This is important if you want to photograph them.

Water

Don't forget that birds need water. You can supply it in a shallow dish or an up-turned dustbin lid supported on some bricks. A night-light placed under the dish should keep the water ice-free in winter.

What to feed

LEFT-OVERS

Scraps from your own meals are fine, although birds are not keen on vegetables other than potatoes. Fat trimmed from bacon and other meat before cooking is a good source of energy, as is uncooked pastry.

BIRD PUDDING

You can make this easily by adding left-over scraps to a bowl of melted lard or dripping, together with breakfast cereals, uncooked porridge oats, crushed peanuts, seeds, dried fruit and grated cheese. When set, turn out the pudding and place on the bird table in a solid mass, or pack it into a small flower pot or half a coconut shell and hang it upside-down.

Tits are the main visitors to terra cotta bells. They can be filled with bird pudding, either purchased ready-made or cooked up in your kitchen. Remember to wash the bells before refilling them.

BONES FROM THE WEEKEND JOINT

Hang these up to attract tits and starlings. Be sure to remove the bones after two or three days to prevent the build-up of potentially harmful bacteria.

SEEDS AND DRIED FRUIT

Finches and other seed-eaters are happiest with a variety of seeds and dried fruit. You can buy wild bird mixtures but avoid ones with a high proportion of cereal-based products as they do not provide enough energy for birds during cold weather. You can collect seeds from teasels, plantains, dandelions and other plants. If you dry them well and store them in a dry place they will remain in good condition for several months. Pine cones yield useful amounts of seed. You can also collect acorns, beechnuts and hazel nuts.

With their high fat or oil content, sunflower seeds are excellent for many garden birds. The black seeds are especially nutritious and their relatively thin husks mean that the birds do not have to expend a lot of energy opening them.

PEANUTS

Shelled peanuts are traditionally presented in a net or a basket, but you can wedge them into holes drilled in small logs. Hang the logs in a tree and watch the tits, woodpeckers and nuthatches trying to dig them out. In their shells, they can be threaded on to lengths of fine wire and hung from branches. Great tits and finches will soon discover what is inside the shells. Salt is bad for birds, so never put out salted peanuts.

FRESH COCONUT

This is another favourite food, best served in the shell. Cut the nuts in half and hang each half upside-down from a convenient support; blue tits and great tits will have a swinging time as they chip away at the flesh with their beaks. Never give birds desiccated coconut for it has a nasty habit of swelling up inside them.

Robins are particularly fond of bird pudding. The fat gives them plenty of energy in the cold winter months.

When to feed

It was once thought that birds should be given additional food only during the winter, but most ornithologists now recommend feeding them right through the year. Apart from encouraging the birds to stay in and around your garden, this will improve their breeding success. Although nestlings are usually given their natural food, the adults are happy to eat the additional food that we supply, thereby freeing more natural food for the nestlings.

Once you have started to feed your garden birds, keep it up and try to feed them at a fixed time each day. Otherwise, birds that have come to depend on you might hang around all day instead of going off to forage; this could be fatal in the winter.

BIRD FEEDERS

You can buy a range of bird feeders from garden centres, pet shops and specialist dealers, including the RSPB (see page 188). Some are very ingenious with 'serving hatches' and domes that can be moved up and down depending on the size of the birds you wish to attract. Hung from trees or walls or attached to your bird table, feeders will hold and dispense peanuts and seed mixtures very efficiently. Some are even designed to keep out squirrels!

PLANTS FOR BIRDS

Most of our garden birds originally inhabited woodland clearings and margins, so our hedge-lined gardens, with their trees and shrubberies, are home from home for them. They provide food, nesting sites and song posts from which the birds can defend their territories and advertise for mates.

NATIVE TREES

Many native trees are worthy of a place in a small garden, but try to get seedlings or saplings from your own area. This should ensure that they grow well and eliminate any risk of contaminating the gene pool with alien genes. It is worth contacting your local Wildlife Trust; many nature reserves sell saplings that

The coal tit, easily identified by the white patch on the back of its black head, breeds mainly in coniferous woodland, but will scour a wide range of deciduous and evergreen garden trees searching for insects and spiders in the winter.

The guelder rose has large plates of fragrant cream flowers in early summer, followed by shiny red bird-friendly berries.

are removed during the winter management work. If you have room for only one tree and your soil is fairly light, a silver birch could be ideal. Tits and other birds enjoy its abundant small seeds, and feed on its huge insect population. It supports over 200 insect species in Britain alone. For damp soils, the common alder takes a lot of beating. It has a beautiful shape and, although it lacks autumn colour, the male catkins give it a fine purple tinge in the winter. Its cone-like fruits yield a good supply of seeds for finches and other birds.

Other good trees include hazel, whose nuts attract plenty of birds and squirrels, bird cherry, rowan, crab apple, dogwood, guelder rose, buckthorn and spindle. If you grow apples or pears, then leave some of the windfalls out for the birds. Blackbirds and starlings really like them, and if you keep some of the fruit back for the winter, then you might attract some fieldfares and redwings as well.

Where to plant trees

Plant the trees in small clumps if you have room for more than one, and try to plant them on the north side. This will give your garden some protection from the coldest winds and provide a sheltered, sunny spot for some woodland-edge plants, such as bluebells and foxgloves. It will also create a sunny spot in which to sit and watch your garden visitors. You can scatter some chipped bark or leave a few logs under the trees to give the area a more natural look.

Trees and shrubs for nests

The trees that are mentioned above provide plenty of food for birds but, although the collared dove may be tempted to fix its flimsy platform to the branches, most birds prefer to nest in something more compact. Holly is good, especially if you plant a berry-bearing specimen that will provide food as well; whitebeam is a particularly good choice in town and city gardens.

Hawthorn, blackthorn, firethorn, *Stranvaesia (Photinia) davidii*, *Rosa rugosa* and various cotoneasters are all worth planting, either as specimen shrubs or as part of a hedge. Don't be too eager to trim them and your reward will be a wealth of colourful autumnal fruits. In any case, do not trim the branches until the birds have finished nesting.

USEFUL CLIMBERS

Boston ivy, also known as Virginia creeper, is grown on houses for its brilliant autumn colours. The dense foliage provides plenty of cover for birds during the summer, and it is well worth installing a few nest boxes among the branches. Climbing hydrangea, which flourishes on shady walls, will also offer plenty of shelter to garden birds. Let honeysuckle, wild roses, brambles and the various forms of *Clematis montana* run wild over shrubs or hedges. Blackbirds and thrushes will nest among them and will particularly enjoy their fruits and seeds in the autumn.

In addition to providing food and safe nesting sites for the birds, fragrant climbing honeysuckle will scent your whole garden on summer evenings.

Bountiful ivy

Many gardeners ruthlessly remove ivy in the belief that it is a tree-killing parasite. It can weaken trees by competing with them for water, minerals and light, and its dense evergreen foliage can severely damage a hedgerow, but it is not a true parasite. Keep it under control by regular trimming and you will find that its benefits far outweigh any disadvantages, as it can feed and shelter a wonderful array of wildlife.

Robins, flycatchers, dunnocks and many other birds nest and roost in the foliage; the flowers will yield abundant nectar for butterflies and other insects preparing for hibernation in the autumn; and the fruits can be life-savers for thrushes and other birds searching for food in the spring.

Ivy berries are among the few fruits that ripen in the spring, making them a valuable food source for garden birds.

HERBACEOUS DINNER TABLES

Sunflowers are often covered with bees and other insects, and when the flowers fade greenfinches and goldfinches flock to feast on the nodding seed heads. If the birds allow any seeds to ripen, collect them and use them on the bird table during the winter. Teasels, cultivated thistles, poppies, cornflowers and love-in-a-mist all attract goldfinches, which sway precariously on the stems while digging out seeds – often long before they are ripe. You could even cultivate a patch of dandelions and let them seed for these birds.

The tubular central florets of the sunflower are full of scent and nectar. When the bees have done their work, each flowerhead contains hundreds of nutritious seeds.

ROBINS

The robin's song, boldness and cheery appearance have long endeared it to us, and, indeed, it is usually regarded as Britain's national bird.

COURTSHIP

Males and females sing and display with equal vigour, and for several months each bird remains fiercely independent, even attacking any other robin that dares to encroach upon its territory. As autumn turns to winter, females are allowed into the males' territories.

A robin will quickly learn to take mealworms from your hand. Offer the worms on the ground in front of you at first.

'Engaged' pairs may feed close to each other, but otherwise have little contact until the spring. The male continues to defend his territory with song, but the female gradually stops singing and gets ready for the breeding season. She builds the nest unaided in the spring, choosing a fairly low, dark hole if possible.

Nesting

Leaves and moss form the bulk of the cup-shaped nest, which is then lined with fine roots and hair. There is usually no shortage of nesting materials in a normal garden, but if you hang up a bag of moss, wool and hair, you will be able to enjoy watching the hen robin tugging out the pieces and cleverly manipulating them with her beak before flying back to her nest. Breeding usually starts in March or April and the robins may raise two or even three broods during the next three or four months.

While the female is building the nest and incubating the eggs, the male feeds her regularly. This courtship feeding is easy to watch once you have located the female. If you maintain a feeding station, the male will return to it every few minutes throughout the day.

You can make it easier for your robins by providing a ready-made home. An open-fronted box, hidden in a dense hedge or on an ivy-clad wall, is ideal.

BLUE TITS

Easily identified by the bright blue crown, blue tits are present in virtually every British garden, especially in the winter when dozens of blue tits pass through each day, staying just long enough for a snack.

DIET AND NESTING

Blue tits are essentially insectivorous birds, using their tiny pointed beaks to pluck caterpillars, aphids and many other insects from trees in summer. In winter,

The blue tit is a sharp-eyed hunter. It is able to spot the tiniest of insect eggs in bark crevices and pluck them out with its tweezer-like beak.

they scour tree trunks and branches for aphid eggs and spiders, although seeds are more important at this time. Like other tits, the blue tit is an inquisitive bird and readily finds and adapts to new sources of food. The birds display amazing agility while taking peanuts from a variety of feeders, and their habit of pecking through milk bottle tops to get at the cream is equally well known.

Blue tits are hole nesters and, like great tits, they will readily nest in traditional tit boxes. The female builds the nest, using plenty of moss and hair or wool, and she incubates the eggs while the male works hard to keep her supplied with a diet of juicy caterpillars.

The great tit is distinguished from the blue tit by its larger size and black crown on the head.

HOUSE SPARROWS

If you live in a town you might think house sparrows are one of our commonest birds, but this is far from the truth. Distinguished by the dull grey crown, they are rarely seen far from human habitation, and huge tracts of the countryside have none at all.

DIET AND NESTING

House sparrows are sociable birds and where they occur they are often seen in large numbers, feeding on seeds and scraps they can glean from streets and

The black bib of the male house sparrow is smaller in winter. Female house sparrows have no bib at all.

The tree sparrow differs from the house sparrow in having a chestnut crown and white cheeks with a black patch in the middle.

gardens. Although basically ground-feeding, they are perfectly happy on the bird table and are quite good at extracting peanuts from various feeders.

House sparrows usually nest in small colonies, with several pairs of birds living on a few neighbouring properties. The rest of the street may have no nests at all, although the sparrows may feed there.

The untidy nests are made of grass and straw but also include wool and feathers. Nests are usually built on houses, especially creeper-clad walls, or in dense hedges, and the birds appreciate open-fronted boxes or tunnels (see page 131) fixed in sheltered spots. A colony may exist for several years but then, for no obvious reason, leave and settle in another part of town.

IDENTIFYING GARDEN BIRDS

Bullfinch (male)

Identification: Male has black head, rosy underparts and white rump in flight. Female is similar but duller.
Distribution: Resident everywhere.
Feeding habits: Buds, often removed from our fruit trees and bushes, form up to 30 per cent of its diet in the spring. Soft fruit is attacked later in the year, so the bird is not usually welcome in the garden.
Nest: Usually low in a thick hedge or bush.
Notes: Birds mate for life; usually seen in pairs.

Siskin (male)

Identification: Yellow rump and tail flashes seen in flight. Female lacks male's black cap and bib and is streaky grey below.
Distribution: Resident in wooded areas, but mainly a winter visitor to gardens.
Feeding habits: Particularly fond of the seeds of conifers and alders but readily takes peanuts from the bird table.
Nest: Usually high in coniferous trees.
Notes: Increasingly common in British gardens in winter.

Chaffinch (male)

Identification: Look for the broad white shoulder flash and wing bar. Male has slate-blue head and rust-red face (less bright in winter than summer). The female is much browner.

Distribution: Resident everywhere.

Feeding habits: A regular visitor to gardens, but more often seen scouring ground below than perching on the bird table

Nest: Neat cup of moss and lichen wedged into a tree or shrub.

Notes: One of Britain's commonest birds.

Greenfinch (male)

Identification: Narrow yellow edge to wing. Male has greyish-green back; female has brown tinge and dark streaks. Both show yellow tail flashes in flight.

Distribution: Resident almost everywhere.

Feeding habits: Takes seeds from trees and herbaceous plants. Very partial to peanuts. Also eats buds.

Nest: A bulky cup wedged in the fork of a tree or tall shrub, usually some kind of conifer.

Notes: Often forms small flocks in winter.

Goldfinch

Identification: Red face and golden wing bars. The sexes are alike.
Distribution: Resident almost everywhere.
Feeding habits: Feeds mainly on the seeds of herbaceous plants, often balancing acrobatically on the flower-heads to pull out the unripe seeds. It also takes crushed seeds from the bird table.
Nest: A neat cup built in a tree or tall shrub.
Notes: Most common in gardens in late summer and autumn, when the birds may form flocks.

Wren

Identification: Plump and rounded, with tail often distinctively cocked. Look for prominent eye-stripe and dark bars on wings and tail. Sexes are alike.
Distribution: Resident almost everywhere.
Feeding habits: Eats insects and spiders and also takes crumbs from under the bird table.
Nest: A ball of moss and leaves, usually built in some kind of hole: sometimes nests in tit-boxes.
Notes: Britain's commonest bird although not the most common of our garden birds. Often mistaken for a mouse as its scuttles through the undergrowth.

Collared dove

Identification: Black collar on delicate pinkish-grey plumage. Sexes are alike.
Distribution: Resident almost everywhere.
Feeding habits: A grain-eater; enjoys vegetable foods but rarely feeds other than on the ground.
Nest: A flimsy platform of twigs, usually in a tree.
Notes: Almost unknown in Europe 100 years ago but now occurs almost all over the continent and its monotonous coo-cooo-cu can be heard in nearly every garden.

Jackdaw

Identification: The grey neck distinguishes it from other members of the crow family. The sexes are alike.
Distribution: Resident almost everywhere.
Feeding habits: Omnivorous, often seen tugging worms and insect grubs from lawns. It may kill and eat nestlings of other birds. Eats fruit, especially cherries.
Nest: An untidy accumulation of twigs, lined with wool and assorted plant fibres and usually built in a hole. Chimneys are often used, as are large open-fronted nest boxes.
Notes: The birds mate for life and are usually seen in pairs.

Pied wagtail (male)

Identification: Look for long tail, white forehead, and black crown. Female is greyer. Throat of both sexes white in winter.

Distribution: Resident in much of Western Europe: summer visitor only in north and east.

Feeding habits: Insectivorous, often snapping up insects on lawns or by ponds. Takes crumbs from bird table in winter.

Nest: In holes, often in dry stone walls: may use open-fronted boxes if these are well concealed.

Notes: Named for the vigorous wagging of its long tail.

Starling

Identification: Black with strong purple and green iridescence and pale spots that are most obvious in winter and gradually disappear in spring. Bill is yellow in summer, brown in winter. Young birds are dull brown. Starlings strut over the ground and do not hop in the way that most other garden birds do. The sexes are alike.

Distribution: Resident almost everywhere.

Feeding habits: Omnivorous, fond of fallen apples in autumn.

Nest: Usually in a hole in a wall or a tree.

Notes: Forms huge roosting flocks in winter.

House martin

Identification: Look for black back, white rump, pure white underparts, and short, forked tail. The sexes are alike.

Distribution: Summer visitor to all of Europe, but most common around human habitation.

Feeding habits. Insectivorous, most often seen catching flies and other small insects in full flight high above the garden.

Nest: Mud cup fixed to cliffs and walls, under eaves of buildings. May also use appropriately shaped boxes (see page 130).

Notes: Providing mud and feathers may encourage the birds to nest on your house.

Swallow

Identification: Look for the red face and throat and the long forked tail. The sexes are alike.

Distribution: Summer visitor to all of Europe; most common around farms and villages.

Feeding habits: Insectivorous, catching small insects in mid air, although usually flying at lower levels than house martin and often just above the ground.

Nest: A cup of mud and feathers, usually built on a ledge in or on a building.

Notes: Often drinks while skimming over the water surface.

Fieldfare

Identification: Look for the grey head and the heavily streaked buff breast. The pale grey rump is very conspicuous in flight. The sexes are alike.

Distribution: Breeds in northern and central Europe, but is a winter visitor to most other parts.

Feeding habits: Scours gardens and hedgerows for fruit in winter and may come to the bird table. Worms and insects are eaten in summer.

Nest: A bulky cup of mud and grass, built anywhere from the ground to the tree tops.

Notes: Forms large flocks in cold winters.

Spotted flycatcher

Identification: Greyish-brown back and dirty white underparts which are streaked with brown. The sexes are alike.

Distribution: Summer visitor to all of Europe.

Feeding habits: Catches a variety of insects by darting out from a perch and snapping them up in mid-air. It usually returns to its perch to eat.

Nest: In holes or on ledges; readily uses open-fronted boxes.

Notes: May be confused with the dunnock (see page 123), but the latter is browner and has red legs.

Blackbird (male)

Identification: Male is glossy black with a yellow bill. Female is dark brown with faint spotting on the breast and a brown bill.

Distribution: Resident in most parts of Europe, but only a summer visitor in the north.

Feeding habits: Omnivorous, but especially fond of earthworms and fruit; a regular visitor at, or more often under, the bird table.

Nest: In shrubs, hedgerows and creepers; made largely with grass and mud.

Notes: One of Britain's commonest birds.

Song thrush

Identification: Look for plain brown back and buff and white underparts marked with more or less triangular black spots.

Distribution: Resident in most of western Europe, but only a summer visitor in the north.

Feeding habits: Omnivorous, taking fruit and earthworms as well as visiting the bird table. Snails are a favourite food and birds can often be heard smashing the shells against stones.

Nest: Built with grass and mud in shrubs, hedges and creepers.

Notes: Mistle thrush is greyer with more rounded spots.

Great spotted woodpecker

Identification: Look for the deep red patch under the tail and the large white wing patch. Only the male has a red spot at the back of the head.
Distribution: Resident in wooded areas almost all over Europe but not in Ireland.
Feeding habits: Digs insects from tree trunks and eats nuts and seeds. Delights in removing peanuts you care to wedge into bark crevices.
Nest: A hole excavated in a tree trunk; will use tit boxes after enlarging the opening.
Notes: Lesser spotted woodpecker is much smaller; male has a red crown but there is never any red underneath.

Green woodpecker

Identification: Red crown and green back. Sexes are alike.
Distribution: Resident in most wooded parts of Europe except Ireland and far north.
Feeding habits: Sometimes digs insects from tree trunks, but is usually seen quartering the lawn in search of ants.
Nest: A hole in a tree trunk.
Notes: Loud, chuckling call has earned alternative name of yaffle.

Nuthatch

Identification: Blue-grey crown and back, rusty brown underparts and black eye-stripe. The sexes are alike.
Distribution: Resident in most of Europe, but not Ireland or northern Britain.
Feeding habits: Digs insects and spiders from bark crevices and wedges in hazel nuts before hammering them open with its sturdy beak.
Nest: In tree holes, but readily accepts tit boxes.
Notes: The only bird that can run down a tree trunk as easily as it can climb up.

Dunnock

Identification: Streaky brown back and sides, with a greyish head and breast, although it often looks streaky brown all over. Beak is slender and legs are reddish. Sexes are alike.
Distribution: Most of Europe, but only a summer visitor in the north.
Feeding habits: Mainly insectivorous, nearly always feeding on the ground.
Nest: A stout cup, usually in a dense bush or hedge.
Notes: Sometimes called a hedge sparrow because of its dull brown colour, but it is not related to the true sparrows.

HOUSES FOR BIRDS

Feeding the birds in your garden can provide them with a vital lifeline in the winter and can give you a great deal of fun as well, so why not go a step further and actually give the birds somewhere to live?

You can then enjoy watching the parents building their nests and feeding the young, and later you will be able to watch the young birds learning to fly. Many birds readily take to nest boxes, especially if natural sites are in short supply – as they often are in small and new gardens.

MAKING A NEST BOX

This is actually very easy – you don't even have to be good at carpentry, just able to saw fairly straight and glue, screw or nail a few pieces of wood together. The birds will probably appreciate the ventilation produced by a few gaps, so do not worry about achieving perfection. The two basic types of nest box (the traditional tit box, beloved by blue tits and great tits and also by wrens and nuthatches, and the open-fronted box, favoured by robins and flycatchers) can both be made from a single plank of wood, as shown in the diagrams opposite.

Wildlife project: making a tit box

Use rough sawn timber about 15 cm (6 in) wide, 145 cm (57 in) long and 18 mm (³/₄ in) thick and cut it as shown. The entrance hole is best at one side; if you do not want house sparrows to get in it should be no more than 28 mm (just over 1 in) in diameter. This will allow tits to get in, plus wrens and nuthatches.

Side-entrance tit box

The hinge can be formed from thick polythene or some rubber inner tube. Put a couple of small drain holes in the base. Protect the box with non-toxic paint or varnish before you put it together: not creosote or similar preservatives. An open-fronted box can be made in the same way but with the front panel only one-third to one half of the height.

Open-fronted robin box

Entrance hole

| Side | Side | Front |

| Back | Top | Floor |

Decide where you are going to site your tit box before you make the entrance hole, and then make sure that it is on the right side: where you can see it but away from the prevailing wind. The latch is not essential, but it does prevent the lid from lifting in a strong wind.

You can buy a wide range of 'designer' boxes from pet shops and other suppliers. Don't be tempted by fancy, colourful boxes – the birds will prefer natural materials and colours. Avoid plastic boxes also as they will overheat and sweat in the summer.

WHEN AND WHERE

Don't wait until the nesting season to put up your boxes; get them into position well before Christmas so that the birds have plenty of time to get used to them. Wrens, tits and other small birds may well roost in the boxes on cold winter nights.

Tit boxes

These can be fixed to walls and tree trunks, sheltered from the full sun so that the eggs and babies won't be cooked. Make sure that the boxes are firmly fixed and cannot sway in the wind.

Open-fronted boxes

These always need to be concealed among climbing plants on a wall or a pergola, or otherwise securely fixed in a hedge.

Nest box guidelines

All boxes must be high enough to be out of reach of cats, preferably more than 2 m (6 ft) above the ground. You might like to fix some kind of landing platform close to the box. The birds will not always use it, but if they do you will get a better view of what food and nesting materials they bring in. You will also have a much better chance of photographing your guests.

Apart from house sparrows and house martins, most of our garden birds are territorial and they spread their nests out so that they can all get enough food for their young. So, although several different kinds of birds may use your nest boxes, you should not expect more than one pair of each species to nest in a small garden.

Nesting materials

Hang up net bags stuffed with building materials at the beginning of the nesting season and watch the birds collect what they need. The easier it is for them to collect nesting material, the more likely they are to nest in your garden. Wool, string, feathers and straw are all suitable, and it is worth adding a handful of hair, easily obtained from your hairdresser's floor. Avoid brightly coloured materials, which might make a nest more conspicuous to predators.

Open-fronted nest boxes need more shelter than tit boxes. Place them in creepers on a wall or tree trunk or under the eaves. This one is being used by spotted flycatchers.

Made from a mixture of wood and cement, Schwegler boxes come in a wide range of designs, which are suitable for all kinds of birds. Tough and long-lasting, they also have remarkable insulating properties that cut down temperature fluctuation inside and reduce the problem of condensation.

This tit box has an anti-predator device. Squirrels, cats and other predators are amazingly clever at reaching nest boxes that you think are out of their reach, and they kill lots of nestling birds. This simple device fitted around the entrance hole prevents the predators from reaching into the box and getting at the nestlings.

Specialist boxes

House martins may fix their mud cups tight up under the eaves of your house if there is a handy supply of mud. Encourage them by using artificial nests made from papier-mâché. If they do not move into this accommodation, they may build close to it, and once you have one or more nests, the birds will probably return every year. A bowl of sticky mud is a further inducement to nesting, especially if there are no

These white storks have built their untidy nest on a specially erected platform on top of a house. The birds usually return to the same site each year, adding fresh material each time, so old nests reach enormous proportions.

convenient natural supplies. House martin colonies make a mess with their droppings, but you can place a shelf under the nests and scrape off the 'guano'.

TUNNEL BOXES

Fixed under eaves, these are ideal for house sparrows. Little more than elongated, open-fronted boxes, the tunnels can be made with two short planks screwed or glued together and fixed into a corner so there is just one opening. Larger tunnels, closed at one end and securely fixed in trees, may attract tawny owls. If you can fix an old tea chest high in a barn you can look forward to playing host to a family of barn owls.

In many parts of the continent, it is worth putting up a platform for white storks, whose huge nests often have sparrows squatting in the lower levels.

Strapped to the underside of a large branch, a wooden tube, 75 x 20 cm (30 x 8 in), may attract a pair of tawny owls if you are lucky.

PART FOUR

Reptiles and amphibians

Amphibians are represented in gardens by frogs, toads and newts. All have thin, mucus-covered skin and are confined to damp places. All are carnivorous, feeding on worms, slugs and a wide range of invertebrates. They sleep through the winter in compost heaps and log-piles, or in the mud at the bottom of ponds. The reptiles found in gardens are mainly lizards and snakes. These animals are covered with scales but are never slimy. Most of them prefer drier and warmer places than amphibians and they need to warm up by basking in the morning sunshine before they get going. They are most common in the south.

Tree frogs

Bright green tree frogs breed in many garden ponds in southern and central Europe. They have also been introduced into England.

LIZARDS

Three lizard species are native to the British mainland, but only the common or viviparous lizard and slow worm are likely to occur in gardens. Both are carnivorous, eating insects, spiders and other invertebrates.

THE VIVIPAROUS LIZARD

This is a sun-loving creature and a good way of attracting it to your garden is to leave areas of short grass or bare ground or, better still, a few rocks on which it can sunbathe. Basking is especially important for this lizard because the females give birth to active young and they need warmth for their development. Most other lizards lay eggs. Dry stone walls and log

This common or viviparous lizard is basking in the sunshine on the warm surface of a log.

piles are also good places for the lizards, as long as they get some sunshine. They provide warm surfaces for basking, and their numerous nooks and crannies are ideal sleeping and breeding quarters.

THE LEGLESS LIZARD

The slow worm is often mistaken for a small snake, but this legless lizard is easy to recognize by its uniform shiny brown colour. Its oval eye, equipped with eyelids, is also different from the circular eyes of snakes. Not keen on sunshine, it is usually seen in the evening or after a shower, when slugs are most active. It hunts for

Early morning is a good time to lift slow worm shelters. This is often an ideal opportunity to get a good look at the animals when they are still quite cool and lethargic.

them in hedge bottoms and long grass at the bases of walls and trees, so try to leave patches of grass for this helpful guest. You may also find it in the compost heap, where it enjoys warmth as well as plenty of slugs.

You can encourage slow worms to take up residence in a rough part of the garden by laying down a few pieces of old carpet or some curved roof tiles. These make ideal shelters for slow worms because the animals can get comfortably warm without actually exposing themselves to the sun. Lift the shelters occasionally to see the animals; unlike snakes and other lizards, they tend to sit tight when disturbed and are easy to examine. Slow worms give birth to active young and you may find the babies – like shiny pieces of string – under the shelters in the autumn.

CONTINENTAL LIZARDS

Continental gardens and those in the Channel Islands also support green and wall lizards. With a body 12 cm (5 in) long and a tail up to twice as much again, the green lizard is one of our largest species. Each defends a territory, often a large clump of grass or dense vegetation on which it can bask. The lizards are very touchy and all you usually see is a tail disappearing into the undergrowth. Wall lizards are much easier to watch. Living in and around our houses, they bask on any sunny surface and scamper up and down walls with amazing agility. Give them some old tiles to bask on and, as long as you don't move too quickly, you will be able to watch them quite easily.

The green lizard is easily recognized. Adults are a brighter green than the immature individual shown here.

True to its name, the wall lizard is a great climber, running up and down walls with equal ease and snapping up any spider or insect that comes within its range.

FROGS, TOADS AND NEWTS

These are amphibians, spending part of their life in water and part on land. On land they have to stay in damp places as their thin skins are not waterproof.

ESTABLISHING A COLONY

These always live on land in the summer. They are active mainly at night and find their way into many gardens. Frogs eat slugs and small snails, together

The smooth skin and dark patch behind the eye distinguish the common frog – the only one likely to be found in British gardens – from the common toad (opposite).

This common toad has typically warty skin. Despite their long back legs, toads tend to crawl rather than leap.

with worms, woodlice and a wide variety of insects. Because the animals have to return to the water to breed, installing a pond is the best way to encourage them to stay around in your garden.

Frogs and newts may colonize your pond as soon as it is installed and breed there in its first spring, but toads are extraordinarily faithful to the ponds in which they grew up and are more likely to struggle across a kilometre of countryside to get back home rather than settle down in a new pond. Therefore the best way to establish a toad colony in your garden is to scrounge some spawn or tadpoles from a neighbouring pond with a good population.

Sleeping through the winter

Short days and falling temperatures in autumn stimulate our amphibians to find safe hideaways where they can sleep through the winter. Most of them burrow into the ground or leaf litter, but log piles and compost heaps are equally acceptable. Clusters of frogs, toads and newts may all pile into the same safe shelter. Newts and frogs may also sleep at the bottom of a pond: being dormant, they can get enough oxygen from the water as long as there are not too many dead leaves around them. Rotting leaves use up a lot of oxygen, so remove most of the debris from the bottom of your pond in the autumn.

This male common newt is in full breeding dress, but his colours will fade and his tail fins will shrink when the breeding season is over.

Conservation tip

The great crested or warty newt may turn up in your pond. This largely black newt, up to 15 cm (6 in) long, is strictly protected and you must not disturb it in any way. Just enjoy having one of our rarities as a guest, remembering that it is doing good in your garden even if it does eat some of your frog tadpoles – there are usually far more than your pond can support.

Don't leave it until the winter or you will disturb and possibly kill the sleeping animals.

Balletic newts

Newts lack voices and, instead of grabbing the first female to come along, the male courts the female with an elegant dance, fluttering his fine crest and frilly tail, both of which enlarge at the start of the breeding season. The dancing may last for many hours and is easy to watch in a garden pond.

There is no mating; once the male newt feels that his dancing has sufficiently impressed the female, he drops a packet of sperm and she picks it up in her genital opening. Over the following few weeks she lays 200 to 300 eggs, wrapping each one carefully in a leaf. Whereas frogs and toads leave soon after mating, newts may stay in the water for much of the summer.

A FROG'S LIFE

Waking from its winter sleep, a frog turns its attention to breeding. Its first objective is to find some water and it can travel as far as a kilometre to reach it. Males arrive first, and their noisy choruses can be heard for weeks.

Mating

A female frog, on entering the water, is immediately grabbed by a male, who locks his front legs across her chest. The pair may stay like this for a week or more, and you may see two males locked on a single female. Fertilization takes place in the water; the male releases his sperm as up to 2,000 little black eggs stream from the female's body. The jelly around each egg absorbs water and swells up to form a familiar mass of spawn. Because all the females in a pond spawn at about the same time, the pond may turn into a mass of jelly.

Tadpoles

Eggs become comma-shaped in a week or so, and when the jelly liquefies the tadpoles wriggle free. They cling to disintegrating jelly or neighbouring plants before grazing on algae or sucking up debris rich in micro-organisms from the bottom of the pond. A tadpole has external gills at first, like tiny feathers sprouting from its neck, but these are soon replaced by internal gills like those of fishes.

Once the male has gripped his mate in a loving embrace, the pair will swim around until the female has shed her eggs.

GETTING LEGS AND LOSING A TAIL

When it is about six weeks old, the tadpole begins its metamorphosis into a frog. Tiny back legs appear at the base of the tail, followed by front legs. The eyes become more prominent, and the tail is gradually absorbed into the body. Grazing on algae gives way to a diet of animal food. The froglet leaves the water when it is about three months old and hunts for insects and small animals on land. As it grows up, it may move right away from the pond, although always sticking to damp places. If it evades its numerous enemies, it will return to the water to start the cycle again when it is about three years old.

PART FIVE

Insects and other invertebrates

Invertebrates are the 'creepy-crawlies' of the garden. They are totally lacking in bone and what skeletons they have are on the outside of the body, in the form of a shell or a tough, horny coat. They far outnumber the backboned animals, the vertebrates. This teeming assortment of mini-beasts plays a major role in the ecology of the garden, notably as food for larger creatures, but only three major groups are likely to be noticed by the gardener. These are the annelids or earthworms, the molluscs (slugs and snails), and the arthropods (insects and other many-legged creatures). Most of these small animals will find their way into your garden unaided.

Dragonflies

The migrant hawker and other dragonflies may breed in garden ponds in southern Britain.

BUTTERFLIES

Butterflies are the most colourful of all our garden guests. Because they appreciate the same sorts of plants as we do, you can feel free to fill your garden with beds of vibrantly coloured flowers and then sit back and wait for the butterflies to arrive, making it even more colourful.

The ice plant is a good source of nectar for butterflies seeking out an autumn feast before going into hibernation. Here is a throng of small tortoiseshells and a solitary red admiral.

WHICH PLANTS?

Although young butterflies (caterpillars) generally need native plants, on which they have been feeding for generations, adult butterflies are happy with a wide range of exotic and native plants. This is because the sugary nectar on which they feed is much the same in all flowers, but not all cultivated flowers are equally attractive to the insects. Big, showy, double flowers often lack nectar because the nectaries have been replaced by additional petals. The old fashioned cottage garden flowers, with plenty of scent and nectar, are usually the best of the cultivated forms.

Honesty is doubly useful to the orange tip butterfly: the flowers provide energy rich nectar whereas the leaves and seed capsules are a source of food for the caterpillars.

Encouraging butterflies

The 2001 Garden Butterfly Survey, which was organized by Butterfly Conservation, recorded 46 butterfly species in British gardens – just over 70 per cent of the total British species – although the average gardener will be lucky to see more than about 15 or so regular visitors. You can, however, increase the numbers of both species and individuals by growing the right kinds of plants, which should be massed where possible and situated in full sunlight. Different varieties often have different flowering times, and thus by planting two or more varieties you can increase the period of your garden's attractiveness to butterflies. Regular dead-heading can also prolong the flowering season, but always remember to leave some seeds for the birds.

THE BUTTERFLY BUSH

So strong is the attraction of buddleia for butterflies that it is commonly called the butterfly bush. Many people plant it purely to bring in the butterflies, although it is an attractive plant in its own right. Buddleia has several species, but the various forms of *B. davidii* are the most butterfly-friendly bushes, and those with pale mauve flowers seem to be the best of all. The darker ones, although very striking to look at, often have little nectar and attract far fewer butterflies. *B. davidii* usually flowers from late June until September, but you can extend the flowering

No wildlife garden should be without a buddleia. Even a solitary bush in a town garden will attract butterflies, and you can watch them plunging their long tongues into the nectar-filled tubular flowers. Although unlikely to be seen in British gardens, the swallowtail is common in Europe.

period by tinkering with your pruning regime. Leave one bush more or less unpruned and it will flower somewhat earlier than another which is pruned hard in the normal way in the spring. The globular, orange-yellow flower clusters of the evergreen *B. globosa* open in May – a month or more before *B. davidii* comes into flower – and these will pull in a varied range of early butterflies.

Bramble is an excellent source of nectar for our summer butterflies, including the brimstone shown here.

OTHER BUSHES

Many butterflies are attracted by the heady scent and strong nectar of privet. Bramble is another favourite, providing nectar for the gatekeepers and ringlets. Moth caterpillars also enjoy the foliage. Ivy on a wall or tree will flower in the autumn and provide commas and other autumn butterflies with a good feast of nectar before they go into hibernation. The autumn brood of holly blue caterpillars will also appreciate the flowers and developing fruits.

Caterpillars also need food

Nectar-rich flowers will bring a host of butterflies into your garden, but this does not mean that they will stay and breed because the nectar does not usually come from the plants required by caterpillars. Unfortunately, the caterpillars of most butterflies feed on weeds, including various grasses, but two food plants well worth having in your garden are sweet rocket and honesty. These will feed the adults and young of the orange-tip. If you can find room for a buckthorn bush in your hedge the brimstones will lay some eggs on it.

VITAL STINGING NETTLES

If you want butterflies to breed in your garden, you have to provide the larval food-plants – and for some of our most colourful species, including the peacock and red admiral, this means planting stinging nettles! Ignore the temptation to relegate your nettle patch to a dark corner; the butterflies will ignore it because they like to lay their eggs in sunshine. Cut the patch regularly, a bit at a time, so that there is always some young growth available. And don't be too eager to trim round the bases of trees, walls and hedges; a bit of long grass here may feed the caterpillars of ringlets and gatekeepers.

This caterpillar of the peacock butterfly is on a stinging nettle.

IDENTIFYING BUTTERFLIES

Peacock

Identification: The four eye-spots make it instantly recognizable. Underside almost black.
Flight time: June–October and again in spring after hibernation.
Distribution: All but the far north of Europe.
Food plant: Stinging nettle.
Caterpillar: Black and spiky with numerous white dots.
Notes: A strong-flying migrant.

Brimstone

Identification: Male upperside brilliant yellow; female greenish white. Wings never open at rest.
Flight time: June–September and in spring after hibernation.
Distribution: All but the far north of Europe.
Food plant: Buckthorn and alder buckthorn.
Caterpillar: Blue-green above and lime-green below, with a white stripe on each side.
Notes: Hibernates in shrubs where leaf-like underside gives good camouflage.

Large tortoiseshell

Identification: This is larger than the small tortoiseshell, with no large black patch on the hindwing. The underside is mottled brown.

Flight time: June–August and again in early spring after hibernation.

Distribution: Most of Europe but a rare visitor to Britain.

Food plant: Elm, sallow and other trees.

Caterpillar: Black with orange streaks and spines. Gregarious.

Notes: Becoming rare everywhere.

Small tortoiseshell

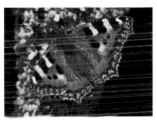

Identification: Look for the blue borders and the extensive black patch at the base of the hindwing. Underside is mottled brown.

Flight time: March–October; usually two broods.

Distribution: All Europe.

Food plant: Stinging nettle.

Caterpillar: Bristly black or dark brown with dense white dots and yellowish sides.

Notes: One of Britain's commonest garden butterflies.

Comma

Identification: Jagged wing margins readily identify this species, named for the comma-shaped white mark under the hindwing.
Flight time: June–September and

again in spring after hibernation; two broods.
Distribution: Most of Europe but not Ireland or Scotland.
Food plant: Stinging nettle, elm and hop.
Caterpillar: Black and orange with a white patch at the rear; spiky.
Notes: Summer butterflies often paler than here.

Red admiral

Identification: Vivid red patches on the velvety black background are unmistakable.
Flight time: May–October.

Distribution: All Europe.
Food plant: Stinging nettle; adult fond of fruit.
Caterpillar: Usually greyish-black but is sometimes paler; always spiny.
Notes: Once thought to be only a summer visitor to Britain, but now seems to hibernate here in increasing numbers, flying early in spring.

Camberwell beauty

Identification: The cream border on wings makes this species unmistakable.
Flight time: June–August and again in spring after hibernation.
Distribution: Most of Europe but only a rare visitor to Britain.
Food plant: Sallow and other deciduous trees.
Caterpillar: Black and spiky with large orange patches on the back.
Notes: Wing margins are paler after hibernation.

Orange tip

Identification: Only male has orange tips; the female is white. Hindwing is mottled green below (page 164).
Flight time: April–June.
Distribution: Through most of Europe
Food plant: Honesty, sweet rocket, garlic mustard and various other crucifers mainly the flowers and seed capsules.
Caterpillar: Bluish-green, speckled with black.
Notes: Rounded wing-tips distinguish female from other whites.

Green-veined white

Identification: Easily recognized by the green lines under the hindwing.
Flight time: March–November; two to three broods.
Distribution: All Europe.
Food plant: Garlic mustard, cuckoo flower, water-cress and various other crucifers; rarely feeds on cultivated brassicas.
Caterpillar: Dull green, speckled with black.
Notes: Summer butterflies have much paler markings than shown here.

Small white

Identification: White upperside has a small black wing-tip and one (male) or two (female) black spots. Hindwing yellow underneath.
Flight time: March–October; two to three broods.
Distribution: All Europe.
Food plant: Numerous wild and cultivated brassicas, and garden nasturtiums.
Caterpillar: Dull green; a yellow stripe on back.
Notes: Summer insects more heavily marked than spring ones.

Large white

Identification: Creamy white above, with large black wing-tip; female has two spots on the upperside of forewing, but male has none.
Flight time: April–October; two broods.
Distribution: All Europe.
Food plant: Mainly

cultivated brassicas but also garden nasturtiums.
Caterpillar: Yellow and black, gregarious for much of their lives.
Notes: Adults are very fond of buddleia.

Small skipper

Identification: Bright orange upperside and orange-tipped antennae. Fast, darting flight and, like many skippers, rests with wings separated.
Flight time: May–August.
Distribution: Southern and central Europe; not Scotland or Ireland.
Food plant: Grasses.

Caterpillar: Pale green with yellow stripes; usually concealed in rolled leaf-blade.
Notes: Essex skipper has black tips to antennae.

Ringlet

Identification: Readily identified by the band of eye-spots on the underside. Upperside is dark brown, sometimes with faint eye-spots.

Flight time: June–August.

Distribution: Most of Europe except far north.

Food plant: Various grasses.

Caterpillar: Pale brown and bristly, with a darker stripe along the middle and a white stripe on each side; two short 'tails'.

Notes: Adult is very fond of bramble blossom.

Swallowtail

Identification: The tails and the black wing bases readily identify this large butterfly.

Flight time: April–September; one to three broods.

Distribution: Most of Europe, but only in Fenland in the British Isles.

Food plant: Various umbellifers, including fennel and wild carrot.

Caterpillar: Plump and green, with black rings and red spots.

Notes: A garden insect only on the continent.

Painted lady

Identification: The wing colour and pattern, with white spots near the tips, is unmistakable.
Flight time: April–October; two broods.
Distribution: A summer visitor to all Europe.
Food plant: Thistles and, less often, stinging nettle and mallow.
Caterpillar: Black and spiky, dotted with white and lined with yellow.
Notes: Probably unable to survive the winter in Europe; migrates from North Africa each spring.

Wall brown

Identification: The eye-spots readily distinguish this from other orange and brown butterflies. The underside of the hindwing is largely grey.
Flight time: April–October; two to three broods.
Distribution: Most of Europe except far north.
Food plant: Coarse grasses.
Caterpillar: Bluish-green with white lines and two short 'tails'.
Notes: Adult butterfly likes to bask on stones and bare ground.

Small copper

Identification: Gleaming coppery forewings and barely-marked brown or greyish underside of hindwings.
Flight time: March–November; two to three broods.
Distribution: All Europe.
Food plant: Common and sheep's sorrel; sometimes docks.
Caterpillar: Bright green with pinkish stripes.
Notes: Strongly territorial, an adult butterfly may defend a clump of flowers all day.

Gatekeeper (or hedge brown)

Identification: There are two white pupils in each eye-spot. Female lacks the dark patch in centre of forewing (seen here in the male).
Flight time: July–September.
Distribution: Southern and central Europe; absent from Scotland.
Food plant: Various grasses.
Caterpillar: Pale brown and bristly, with darker spots, white side stripes and two 'tails'.
Notes: Adult is very fond of marjoram flowers.

Holly blue

Identification: Upperside has a slight violet tinge; male has narower black borders than the female seen here. Underside powdery blue with elongate black spots.

Flight time: April–September; two broods.

Distribution: Most of Europe.

Food plant: Holly and various other shrubs in spring; ivy is main food of autumn brood.

Caterpillar: Pale green with a white side stripe.

Notes: The only blue normally seen in town gardens.

Common blue

Identification: Male is bright violet-blue; female is brown with marginal orange spots. Underside is grey or pale brown with heavy black spots.

Flight time: April–October; two to three broods.

Distribution: All Europe.

Food plant: Bird's-foot trefoil, clovers and other legumes.

Caterpillar: Pale green and bristly, with a white side stripe.

Notes: Mainly rural gardens, mostly as a visitor.

GARDEN MOTHS

The best way to see moths in action is to wander round your garden with a torch after dark. A humid, moonless night is best; you will be surprised by how many moths drift over the flower beds, dropping down to sample the nectar. They will usually visit pale, strongly-scented flowers that show up at night.

CONCEALED OR CONSPICUOUS?

Most of our moths are decidedly sombre in colour, enabling them to rest undetected on fences and tree trunks or amongst the vegetation by day. Some of

A lilac beauty moth blends perfectly with fallen leaves.

The garden tiger moth is extremely conspicuous, and this indicates to birds that it is a very distasteful insect.

their camouflage is truly amazing. They are able to pick out the most suitable backgrounds on which to settle down, and those that resemble bark can even detect the direction of crevices and can shuffle themselves around so that their wing patterns are aligned with those of the bark. Many other moths actually look so similar to twigs or even dead leaves that it takes a really sharp pair of eyes to spot them at rest during the daytime. However, some garden moths are brightly coloured and very conspicuous indeed. This usually indicates that they are distasteful or even poisonous. Tiger moths and magpie moths are good examples. Once they have tasted them, birds quickly learn to leave these brightly-coloured moths alone.

Butterfly or moth?

Colourful moths can be confused with butterflies, but their antennae or feelers will distinguish them. All our butterflies have a little knob on each antenna, whereas most moths' antennae are hair-like or feathery. Almost all moths rest with their wings flat or folded over the body, with only the uppersides visible. Although many butterflies bask with their wings open, almost all of

Feathery antennae are a characteristic of many male moths.

The clubbed nature of a butterfly's antennae are clearly seen in this skipper.

Only the uppersides of the swallowtailed moth's wings are visible at rest.

At rest, only the undersides of the orange tip butterfly's wings are visible.

them rest with their wings closed vertically above the body, so that only the undersides are visible.

Hungry caterpillars

Hundreds of moth caterpillars find our cultivated flowers and vegetables to their liking. In addition to nibbling the leaves, they chew their way through roots and can even be found inside the trunks and branches of trees. Some caterpillars, including those of the mullein and magpie moths, can cause noticeable damage to their food plants, but very few species are sufficiently numerous to spoil the look or the productivity of our gardens.

The larva of the vapourer moth feeds on a wide range of plants and it can damage orchards. Its hairs can cause serious irritation to the skin if it is touched.

IDENTIFYING MOTHS

Brimstone moth

Identification: The butter-yellow wings with brown spots are unmistakable.
Flight time:
April–October; one or two broods.
Distribution: Most of Europe.
Food plant: Hawthorn and many other rosaceous trees and shrubs, including cultivated plums and apples.
Caterpillar: A greyish-brown looper, very twig-like with a twin-pointed hump near the middle.
Notes: Adults readily come to lighted windows.

Lime hawkmoth

Identification: Wings range from green to rusty brown, but always have wavy edges.
Flight time: May–July.
Distribution: Much of Europe except Scotland, Ireland and the far north.
Food plant: Mainly lime, but also elm and alder and some other deciduous trees.
Caterpillar: Pale green with yellow streaks and a horn at the rear.
Notes: Adult lime and eyed hawks do not feed.

Eyed hawkmoth

Identification: Eye-spots on hindwings. Forewings usually pinkish brown. Always a chocolate patch on the thorax.
Flight time: May–September; two broods.
Distribution: Most of Europe, not Scotland.
Food plant: Mainly willows and apple.
Caterpillar: Bluish-green with yellow stripes and a terminal horn; usually rests upside-down.
Notes: The moth scares its enemies by suddenly exposing its eye-spots when disturbed.

Elephant hawkmoth

Identification: Greenish yellow and pink forewings, black and pink hindwings, and white legs readily identify this fast-flying moth.
Flight time: May–July.
Distribution: Most of Europe.
Food plant: Willowherbs, bedstraws and garden fuchsias.
Caterpillar: Dark brown with four eye-spots and a trunk like snout that gives the insect its name.
Notes: Moth often feeds on honeysuckle at dusk.

Barred yellow

Identification: The colour and pattern readily identify this little moth.
Flight time: May–July.
Distribution: Most of Europe except for the far northern areas.
Food plant: Wild and cultivated roses.
Caterpillar: A pale green looper with yellow bands and a dark stripe along the back.
Notes: This hedgerow moth commonly rests with its abdomen pointing upwards.

Golden plusia

Identification: The golden forewings with a silvery figure-of-eight are unmistakable.
Flight time: June–September.
Distribution: Most of Europe, but rarely seen in Ireland.
Food plant: Mainly delphiniums in the garden.
Caterpillar: Leaf green with white spots and lines; only three pairs of stumpy prolegs.
Notes: Caterpillar gnaws through leaf veins, causing leaf to collapse around it like a tent.

ATTRACTING MOTHS

If you have ever left the curtains open in a lighted room on a summer night, you will know that moths are attracted to lights. A stronger light and a white sheet will attract even more moths. Hang the sheet from a washing line, or spread it on the lawn, and shine the light on it. On a warm, overcast night the moths will stream in and will often settle down on the sheet so that you can examine and identify them.

Sweet tongues

Many moths are attracted to a sugary mixture daubed on walls or tree trunks. There are numerous recipes, but rum, beer and molasses usually feature. Mixed to a thick consistency so that it does not run, it should be applied in narrow vertical patches at about head-height. The moths sit around the edges of the meal and push their tongues into it until they have had their fill. Again, you need to sit up late to see them.

Moths attracted by light or sugar will not necessarily be living in your garden, but mated females may stay around long enough to lay eggs on the plants. Most of your visitors, however, will be males, flying around in search of mates and attracted, or perhaps distracted, by your light or sugar patches. The females are usually busy laying their eggs.

Flowers for moths

Pale-coloured flowers that open and release their scent at night provide the best re-fuelling stations for moths, so a moth garden should include night-scented stock, nicotiana (tobacco flower) and honeysuckle. Sweet Williams also attract plenty of moths, but one of the best for attracting the long-tongued hawkmoths is the beauty-of-the-night, which is also known as the marvel of Peru. Its slender, tubular flowers, ranging from white through yellow to red, open their nectar stores in late afternoon. Pussy willow catkins also sustain many moths in the spring.

A convolvulus hawkmoth probes some beauty-of-the-night flowers with a tongue which is about as long as its body.

Wildlife project: trapping moths

If you use a sheet and a lamp, you need to stay up late yourself to see the moths, so you might prefer to use some form of trap around the light. Portable traps, powered by mains electricity or car batteries, can be bought from biological supply companies, but it is not difficult to make a simple trap with a large cardboard box.

1 Cut a hole in the top of the box to take a large plastic funnel, and put several sheets of egg-packing inside.
2 Suspend an ordinary lamp of 150–200 watts directly above the funnel to attract plenty of moths.
3 Moths hitting the light fall through the funnel and into the box, where they settle down comfortably in the hollows of the egg-packing. They can be examined in the morning and released unharmed.
4 The trap can be left on all night, but the lamp must have a transparent shield over it to protect it from rain. Cold rain hitting the hot lamp may cause it to shatter.

Safety tip When using mains electricity, always ensure that all electrical connections are suitable for outdoor use and are well protected from rain and dew.

BEES

Asked to name some bees, most people are likely to come up with just two: the honey bee and the bumble bee. Gardeners may add the leaf-cutter bee, but there are actually over 250 different kinds of bees in the British Isles. The adults feed primarily on nectar and they play a major role in pollinating our wild and cultivated flowers, including fruit crops.

DANCING BEES

On each expedition from its hive, a honey bee tends to visit just one kind of flower, so the pollen is not wasted on flowers where it cannot effect pollination. This makes honey bees particularly good pollinators. Fruit growers often borrow beehives when their trees are in flower to guarantee successful pollination of the blossom and a good fruit crop – and the bee keepers benefit from a good yield of honey, which the bees make from the nectar. The bees are incredibly efficient at collecting nectar because an individual finding a good source tells the rest of the colony about it by 'dancing' when it returns to the hive. The direction and speed of the dance tells the other workers exactly where to find the nectar, and they fly out to gather it.

Copious supplies of nectar and pollen mean that the little hover-fly on the right can feed happily alongside the larger bumble bee on this colourful helichrysum flower.

You can get a reasonably good idea of the efficiency of this recruitment by putting a spoonful of honey or strong sugar solution on a saucer and persuading a bee to drink from it. This is not as difficult as you might think: if you dip a small twig in some honey and hold it close to a bee on a flower, the bee will readily transfer its attention to the honey and you can carry it to the saucer. Mark the bee with a small spot of non-toxic paint while it is feeding and then watch it fly off. As long as its hive is not too far away, you may well find it back with a gang of friends a few minutes later.

HAIRY BUMBLES

Bumble bees are generally bigger and furrier than honey bees. They usually nest in the ground, often in hedge-banks. Only the mated females (queens) survive the winter and they start new colonies in the spring. Bumble bees make no combs and do not store much honey, but they are still important pollinators. Many bumble bee species have become noticeably rarer in recent years. You can help to restore the fortunes of the bees by planting nectar-rich flowers, including the following ones: borage, foxglove, globe thistle, helichrysum, knapweed, lungwort, marjoram, poppies, red clover, red deadnettle, sage and teasel.

Guided by the dark spots, a bumble bee enters a foxglove flower to sample the nectar at the top of the bell. While feeding, the bee will be dusted with pollen, much of which will be carried home in the baskets on its back legs.

LIVING ALONE

Most bees are solitary insects, with each female working alone to make a small nest. Each nest consists of a few cells and may be constructed in the ground, dead wood or hollow stems and other crevices. Leaf-cutter bees make their nests with sections of leaves cut from roses and other plants. Other solitary bees make their nest cells with sand or mud, fibres plucked from plants or sawdust from excavating in wood. The cells are stocked with a mixture of pollen and nectar and an egg is laid in each one. The female seals the cells and flies away. She has no contact with her offspring.

Safety tip
Solitary bees rarely sting us; even the social ones are not usually aggressive as long as you don't stand in front of their nests. Their stings can be painful, but the pain is usually short-

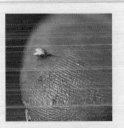

lived. If you are stung by a honey bee the strongly-barbed sting will stay in your skin. Don't pull it out with tweezers, as this will force more poison into you. Scraping it out is a much better way.

The bee hotel

You can attract solitary bees into your garden by constructing a 'bee hotel'. This consists of one or more planks of wood, 10–15 cm (4–6 in) thick, drilled with numerous holes ranging from 2–10 mm ($1/12$–$2/5$ in) in diameter. Fix the planks to a wall or fence in a sheltered, south-facing spot. Watch the bees select their 'rooms' and stock them ready for egg-laying. A large log or tree stump drilled with holes is equally acceptable to bees. With about a quarter of Britain's native bees now listed as endangered species, anything you can do to help must be a good thing.

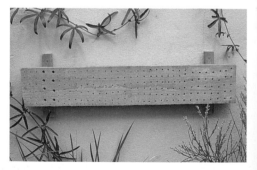

Dozens of solitary bees, of several different species, may take up residence in a simple 'bee hotel', which is made from a thick plank screwed to the wall.

Hollow canes or tubes up to a centimetre in diameter make great homes for solitary bees. Pack them into a tin or a length of drain pipe 15 cm (6 in) long. Make sure that the bees can enter only at one end; if you use a length of drain pipe, you will have to block up the ends of the tubes with modelling wax.

BUMBLE BEE HOMES

Bumble bees usually nest on or under the ground, often in old mouse nests in well-drained banks. They sometimes accept artificial homes, and a simple wooden box with a couple of 15 mm (³/₅ in) holes in the sides makes a good bumble bee home. Stuff it with old mouse or gerbil bedding – scrounged from the pet shop if you have no pets of your own – and bury it in a pile of leaf litter at the base of a hedge so that the holes are just visible. Do this in early spring, when the queens are searching for nest sites. If it is accepted, you will be able to watch the coming and going of the bees throughout the summer. A medium-sized flower pot, buried in a bank with the drain hole just visible, may also be acceptable to bees.

DRAGONFLIES

Despite their fast and often noisy flight, and country names such as 'horse stingers' and 'devil's darning needles', these beautiful, gauzy-winged creatures are harmless and should be welcome in any garden. They catch mosquitoes and troublesome flies and, being among our largest insects, they are easy to watch.

DRAGONS AND DAMSELS

The larger species, which always rest with their wings outstretched, are often called true dragonflies. Their great eyes, with up to 30,000 tiny lenses, can spot the

Azure damselflies display the group's unique mating posture: the male holds the female's neck while she curves her body forward to contact the front of his abdomen.

Breeding in many garden ponds, the large red damselfly is often on the wing in April and is one of the first species to appear in our gardens in the spring.

slightest movement, and their amazing manoeuvrability enables them to change direction instantly to grab their prey in mid air. Victims are scooped up by the spiky legs, which are held under the head like a net. Hawker dragonflies each adopt a territory, such as a hedgerow, and patrol it for hours, snatching prey that comes within range and seeing off other dragonflies, often with a clashing of wings. Darter dragonflies spend most of their time on a perch, from which they dart out to catch passing prey.

The smaller dragonflies, which usually rest with their wings vertically above their slender bodies, are called damselflies. Slower and more delicate, they prefer to pluck aphids and small insects from the vegetation.

Watery beginnings

Dragonflies all grow up in water and, although the larger species may well visit gardens far from water, you are most likely to attract them if you have your own pond. The more sedentary damselflies are unlikely to be seen in your garden unless you or one of your close neighbours has a pond. A good pond will encourage both groups to breed. Ideally, you need some emergent plants that the young insects can climb when about to change into adults and also some floating plants on which the adults can bask. Many species also need vegetation to support them while laying their eggs, and don't forget one or two prominent perches for the darters – canes pushed into the surrounding ground are fine, especially if they overhang the water.

BREEDING

If you see a dragonfly bobbing over the pond surface and periodically dipping its abdomen into the water, it will be a female laying eggs. Some species cling to the vegetation and push their abdomen into the water to lay eggs on or in the submerged stems, and in a number of species the male actually holds the female by the neck while she deposits her eggs. The pair will even fly in this tandem position while looking for suitable sites. You are most likely to see the young stages – the nymphs – when pulling out

Left: A nymph may spend several years in the water before climbing a plant stem and splitting its skin to release the new adult.

Below: The life cycle of the dragonfly begins when the female lays her eggs in the water.

excess vegetation or removing mud from the bottom of the pond in the autumn. Generally dark grey with long legs, they are equipped with a fearsome lower jaw that can be shot out to impale small creatures.

LADYBIRDS

Every gardener can easily recognize a ladybird. These colourful beetles are valuable allies in the constant struggle against aphids and other insect pests. There is not a lot you can do to encourage ladybirds into a garden, but if your roses or other plants are suffering from a plague of aphids try collecting some ladybirds from the wild and put them on the infested plants.

You can buy ladybird cultures, but don't be surprised when you receive bluish-grey grubs instead of the familiar beetles. These are the ladybird larvae. They are common in gardens, but many gardeners do not know what they are and squash them in the belief that they are nibbling the plants. The larvae are just as good at eating aphids as their parents and each one can eat over 100 in a week – perhaps as many as 500 before it turns into an adult to continue the carnage.

Aphids may well kick and struggle, but they are still no match for a colourful ladybird's jaws.

Ladybirds may hibernate in secluded corners, emerging to sun themselves en masse in the spring.

COLOURFUL WARNINGS

The ladybirds' bright colours warn birds and other predators that the insects taste foul. If you handle them, they literally bleed on your hands and leave long-lasting, pungent stains. Birds have only to try one or two before they learn to leave them alone.

Vegetarian ladybirds

Although most of the ladybirds are entirely predatory, there are some vegetarian species, including the 22-spot ladybird. Named after the 22 little black dots on its yellow wing cases, this tiny creature eats mildews and is often to be found on gooseberry and currant bushes in the spring.

SPIDERS

A small garden may well contain several thousand spiders. There will be many secretive, ground-living hunters as well as more familiar web-spinning species.

ATTRACTING SPIDERS

Spiders' webs are extremely effective traps for many flying and crawling insects and, although they clearly claim many harmless and useful creatures, they do account for a lot of pests. The spiders are therefore important components of the garden fauna. They can make a living almost anywhere and there is no need to do anything to encourage them into the garden

The nursery web spider, seen here carrying its egg sac, hunts on plants. It spins a tent-like web to protect its offspring – hence its name.

The zebra spider is one of the jumping spiders and is very common on garden walls and fences where it picks out its insect prey with its huge front eyes and then jumps on to it from a distance of several centimetres.

other than provide a diversity of habitats. The more you create, the more species you are likely to have. They will take up residence in a hedge or log-pile, on a fence, garden wall or rockery and around doors and windows. The little zebra spider is even happy on bare house walls. Apart from a few Mediterranean species that can pack a painful bite, none of our European spiders is harmful to the gardener.

The garden spider spins its more or less circular web on shrubs and fences. It usually spins a new web each day because insects and the wind often break the silk and reduce the web to an ineffective tangle of threads, as seen here.

KEEPING A RECORD

Having created a wildlife garden, and undoubtedly attracted a wide range of fascinating animal visitors, you will hopefully want to keep a record of their comings and goings throughout the year.

Keeping a diary

You need a diary to keep an accurate record. Start as soon as you embark on wildlife gardening and write down what you see each day. If you are starting a garden or a particular feature from scratch, record the stages at which the plants and animals appear. You can appreciate how the community evolves as the garden matures. Record what the animals are doing as well as the dates on which you see them.

A closer look

A well-sited bird table will enable you to watch your feathered visitors with the naked eye, but a pair of binoculars are essential for observing shyer garden birds as well as dragonflies and butterflies. You will need a magnifying glass to watch caterpillars and bees. An old-fashioned reading glass with a short handle can be useful, but for appreciating the beauty of insect eggs and other tiny objects you will need a lens with a magnification of at least x 10.

Film and video

You can take photographs or make videos of the plants and animals around you to create a permanent record of your garden. A bewildering array of modern cameras is now available to you.

Digital cameras can create fantastic pictures, but cameras for transparencies and colour prints are still popular. A single-lens reflex camera, which is fitted with a 90 mm macro lens, allows you to get good close-ups of insects as well as more distant views without changing lenses.

Whatever camera you choose, you need to be able to over-ride the automatic exposure settings, otherwise pale subjects on dark backgrounds will be washed out and vice-versa. You need electronic flash for most close-ups and subjects in shady spots. If you video your garden, try to tell a story – perhaps an account of a year in the garden. Short sequences of activity, such as a hedge turning green in spring, are far more stimulating than a series of 'snap-shots'.

Spread the word

You can show your photographs or films to local garden clubs and wildlife groups. Your enthusiasm can be infectious and this is one of the best ways to encourage others to take up wildlife gardening.

USEFUL INFORMATION

BIRD FOODS, TABLES AND NEST BOXES

CJ WildBird Foods Ltd
The Rea, Upton Magna,
Shrewsbury SY4 4UR
www.birdfood.co.uk

J.E. Haith Ltd
65 Park Street, Cleethorpes,
N.E. Lincolnshire
DN35 7NF
www.haiths.com

The Royal Society for the Protection of Birds
The Lodge, Sandy,
Bedfordshire SG19 2DL
www.rspb.org.uk

WILD FLOWER SEEDS AND PLANTS

Buckingham Nurseries and Garden Centre
Tingewick Road,
Buckingham MK18 4AE

Fothergill's Seeds
Gazely Road, Kentford,
Newmarket,
Suffolk CB8 7QB

National Wildflower Centre
Court Hey Park,
Liverpool L16 3NA
www.wildflower.org.uk

Naturescape
Maple Farm, Coach Gap
Lane, Langer,
Nottinghamshire
NG13 9HP
www.naturescape.co.uk

Y.S.J. Seeds
Kingsfield Conservation
Nursery, Broadenham Lane,
Winsham, Chard,
Somerset TA20 4JF

Yellow Flag Wildflowers
8 Plock Court, Longford,
Gloucestershire GL2 9DW
www.wildflowersuk.com

NATIONAL ORGANIZATIONS

Bat Conservation Trust

15 Cloisters House,
8 Battersea Park Road,
London SW8 4BG
www.bats.org.uk

Butterfly Conservation

Manor Yard, East Lulworth,
Wareham, Dorset BH20 5QP
www.butterfly
conservation.org

Froglife

Mansion House,
27-28 Market Place,
Halesworth, Suffolk IP19 8AY
www.froglife.org

The Green Gardener

47 Strumpshaw Road,
Brundall, Norfolk NR13 5PG

Henry Doubleday Research Association

Ryton Organic Gardens,
Ryton-on-Dunsmore,
Coventry CV8 3LG
www.hdra.org.uk

London Wildlife Trust Centre for Wildlife Gardening

28 Marsden Road,
London SE15 4EE
www.wildlondon.org.uk

USEFUL WEBSITES

www.nhm.ac.uk/science/projects/fff

Find out which wild plants
are native to your area
simply by entering the first
part of your postcode.

www.greenfingers.com

Wildlife gardening tips.

www.which.net/gardeningwhich/advice/wildflowers.html

Gardening Which? website
which has fact sheets
listing native tree, shrub
and seed suppliers. Advice
sheets on Wildflowers for
the Garden and Making
a Mini Meadow are also
available from their
website.

190

Index

INDEX